發揚大雁氣功

楊梅君題

"Fa Yang Dayan Qigong"

"Continue Practice to Advance Dayan Qigong"

Signed by Yang Mei Jun

Dayan Qigong
An Ancient Health System for Today's Modern Life, 3rd Edition
Published by Wen Wu School of Martial Arts

All rights reserved.
Copyright © 2014 by Master Hui Liu

Cover painting by Master Hui Liu

Cover design by Master Hui Liu

Co-Author Shari Chun

No part of this book may be reproduced or transmitted in any form or by any means, electronic or mechanical, including photocopying, recording, or by any information storage and retrieval system, except where permitted by law, without the written permission of the:

Wen Wu School of Martial Arts and Master Hui Liu
10124 San Pablo Avenue
El Cerrito, CA 94530
(510) 524-1057
www.wenwuschool.com

Visit our website or call to inquire about our other products such as the Dayan Qigong Wild Goose Qigong videos that correlate with this book.

Table of Contents

Acknowledgements and Disclaimer	1
Foreword	3
Remarks by Master Y. C. Chiang	5
About Master Hui Liu	9
Introduction	17
General Principles of Dayan Qigong	19
Story: Life and Teachings of Grandmaster Yang Mei Jun	21
Basic Warm Ups and Massage	45
Summary of Dayan Qigong 64 Movements	70
64 Movements: Specific Instructions	71
Hand and Foot Positions	133
Major Points Used in The Set	135
Meditation	137
FAQ's	145
General Considerations	147
Factors Which May Affect Qigong Practice	151
Practice Advice from Master Liu	153
Meridians and Massage Points Explained	157
Tea Ceremony	175
Specialty Foods and Recipes	183
Famous Quotes: Model for Healthy Living	195
Showing Respect Towards the Teacher	197
Testimonials	201
Scripts and Their Translations	211

Acknowledgements

Paintings and Drawings by Master Hui Liu

Editors: Shari Chun, Loc Huynh, Erlene Chiang, John Dyckman

Photographers: Shari Chun

Calligraphy: Grandmaster Yang Mei Jun, Master Y. C. Chiang, Master Hui Liu

Technical Advisors: Master Hui Liu
Erlene Chiang, Ph.D., L.Ac.
Master Y.C. Chiang, Ph.D., O.M.D., C.A.

Disclaimer

Always check with your physician before exceeding your limit of ability in the practice.

Foreword

Qigong represents an important and, in the western world, little understood healing practice. The Dayan (Wild Goose) style of Qigong presented in this book consists of 64 movements that combine what a western-trained physical therapist would recognize as full-range-of-motion exercises with the elements of Traditional Chinese Medicine (TCM). Practicing these movements circulates life energy, or Qi, throughout the 12 basic organs and their meridians and the 8 regulating meridians (channels). In TCM, when the Qi flows freely in a balanced fashion, health is restored, and disease prevented.

As western-trained psychologists, each of us approached our use of Qigong with a skeptical empiricism. As we began to notice improvements in our own health and sense of well-being, and in our fellow students, we became eager to share this complimentary healing system with our colleagues, and with the patients who came to our respective medical centers.

We found that the movements of Dayan Qigong could be taught to groups of patients with disparate medical problems. Some were interested in stress reduction and disease prevention, and some sought adjunctive self-care for diagnosed medical conditions. We have witnessed positive changes in patients that challenge explanation from our western-trained understanding of physiology. But as empiricists, we acknowledge and are pleased by the increased sense of equanimity, stamina, mobility and comfort that our students report.

This book represents an important resource for both students and researchers alike. It clearly explains both the principles and the practice of Dayan Qigong. It will serve as a valuable textbook for students, and especially for those who do not have easy access to in-person teaching. It will allow potential researchers to closely examine the movements, and to understand the TCM, Traditional Chinese Medicine, purpose of each of the movements. It deserves to be in the hands of any serious student of Qigong.

John Dyckman, Ph.D.
Robert Rosenbaum, Ph.D.

Remarks by Master Y. C. Chiang

Qigong is an ancient form of exercise for longevity. It is not only a physical exercise, but also philosophically and scientifically rooted.

Physically, Qigong can stimulate Qi and blood circulation, improve the body's internal balance, and vitalize a person's mind and body. In philosophical terms, Qigong movements are created based on the revolving theory of Tai-Chi, Yin-Yang, five elements and Bagua to promote circulation of Qi and blood. This circulation increases our metabolism, bringing in fresh and new energy, while expelling bad, stagnant Qi.

Dayan Qigong was invented by a venerable monk, Dao An, who lived during the Qin Dynasty. It consists of 2 sets of 64 movements based on the counter balance of five elements and Bagua, combined with the 12 meridians and 365 acupuncture points. Dayan Qigong includes movements, meditations and medical theories. It is the safest, most complete, and most effective Qigong set in China. Its movements are suitable for all ages and gracefully represent the daily rituals of a wild goose. Dayan Qigong set does not cause any imbalances in Qi circulation, or conflict with other Qigong practices. It can cure illness, and further preserve a youthful life and a healthy mind and body.

In today's generation, scientific proof is almost a requirement. Thirty years ago, Grand Grandmaster Yang, Mei-Jun gave a demonstration in front of a group of scientists and researchers. She brought Qi, from her lower *Dantian*, out of her body in a shape of a "ball", and "floated" it in front of the audience. This amazing feat excited the whole world. Grandmaster Yang started practice at the age of 13 and lived until 108 years old.

My wife, Professor Hui Liu, has achieved profundity in studying Dayan Qigong, under the guidance of Grandmaster Yang for over 25 years. Over the years, she has taught thousands of students all over the world, helping them to attain better health. This new book is a collection of knowledge and experience during Hui Liu's practice of Dayan Qigong. I'm honored to be part of it.

Dr. Y.C. Chiang

Grandmaster Yang Mei Jun and Master Hui Liu explaining their experiences in practicing qigong. (1997)

Dayan Qigong
About Master Hui Liu

Hui Ju Liu was born in northern China, in a village, in Hopei providence, 300 miles north of Beijing.

Her father, Ru Tung Liu, had such an ultimate memory that he could memorize a thousand-word article in just 10 minutes, without dropping a single word. He was always praised as the genius in his village. Mr. Liu had been the director of Education Bureau, County Supervisor, etc., but had no interest in pursuing a political career. His interest was in brush painting. He spent 50 years painting plum blossom in depth, yet none of his paintings are the same. He had been honored as the "Master" of plum blossom painting.

Hui Liu's mother, smart and diligent, was known as a cooking expert among her friends and family. She often showed her talent in clothing design, by designing children's' clothing and her own clothes. She was very creative with her designs.

Hui Liu inherited the best from both parents. She had always won 1st place at school since early years. Winning 1st place in China is being the honor student with the highest grade point average. As she grew older, a 20-mile walk between school and home had become her daily routine. She was the only girl who was willing to continue school in her hometown. And she was the only one who was able to study out of town due to her academic achievement.

Hui Liu also showed a strong interest in painting early on. She learned calligraphy at age 7, and brush painting at age 10. She first learned plum blossom painting from her father, then flowers & birds from Master Shao Yu Hsuan at age 14. At age of 18, she was admitted to National Teachers University in Taiwan as 1st place in brush painting. From there, she was exposed to many famous artists and professors who broaden her horizon in art. After earning her B.A. degree, she taught painting at home and various high schools and colleges in Taiwan for many years.

In 1976, Hui Liu and her husband, Dr. Yun-Chung Chiang, and family immigrated to the U.S. residing in El Cerrito, California. Adapting to a new environment, the language barrier, four young children, and elder parents who all needed care and help made Hui Liu's health deteriorate quickly. The onset of menopause, stress, worry, and anxiety were overwhelming.

Grey hair quickly showed, teeth started to loosen; sleep quality was poor, and poor appetite throughout the day. Though she didn't have a glorious full-time job, cooking 3 meals a day, caring for parents, driving the kids to and from school, housework, and helping with her husband's business in her spare time, hardly gave her any rest during

Dayan Qigong
About Master Hui Liu

the day. By the afternoon, she was exhausted, feeling dizzy and weak, and often coughing and sick.

Due to menopause, she had also experienced imbalance psychologically, such as being suspicious, daydreaming, jealousy unable to believe in oneself. It was a fatal period for any family, not a peaceful house, many arguments. Image while the husband was focusing on establishing the business, children are in their teenage years, the wife was exhausted working all day. A home wouldn't be sweet anymore with frequent quarrels and poor communication. A broken family often starts in such a situation. Thinking back, the root causes are an unhealthy body without proper nourishment and adequate exercise, which leads to unhealthy mind, impatience and intolerance.

During this unstable period, she drove her father to San Francisco for a dental visit one day, and stopped at the tollbooth on Bay Bridge. While the car in the front moved forward, she felt her was moving backward instead, and she slammed on the brakes hard trying to stop the car when her car wasn't moving at all. Later on at a stop light, when the light turned green, she felt she was moving backward again while all other cars proceeded passing her. She was so nervous and afraid to drive. But it was impossible without driving for her whole family.

Meanwhile, many martial art teachers from Taiwan and China often came to visit their business, Wen Wu School of Martial Arts. Her thought originally was to find an easy yet effective exercise for her elder parents. In 1978, a practitioner from Beijing came and demonstrated Dayan Qigong. Until then, Qigong had been secretly taught in China, because "Qi" can be cultivated after practice to help and hurt people. Dayan Qigong was first brought to public by Grandmaster Yang Mei Jun in China.

All of the sudden, many other forms of Qigong forms also appeared public, and a wave of Qigong practice had finally unveiled. Hui Liu had followed a few movements during the demonstration; she then felt Qi moving between her fingers immediately. She knew this is the answer to her search. The year after, Hui Liu went to Beijing to visit Grand Grandmaster Yang. Through many obstacles and great difficulties, she finally met the Grand Master in person. Grand Master had corrected every one of her 64 movements personally, and endorsed Hui Liu as her student officially. From then on, it had been a great benefit meeting the Grand Master every visit to China either Hui Liu herself or the students who went along.

Hui Liu's 1st experience in learning Dayan Qigong was a hot and swollen feeling in her palms. Sometimes she could feel cold air between her fingers. Qi also felt like a thin thread moving upward on inside of her legs, sometimes downward on the outside. Sometimes cold, sometimes hot. When she felt the Qi had stop moving, she would experience small problems on her body, maybe a cold or pain. Hui Liu also felt Qi traveling along outside of her arms, but not as often. Later she realized that was Qi moving along the meridians, and the cold air feeling indicates expelling of bad Qi. Often when she stood in the kitchen

Dayan Qigong
About Master Hui Liu

working, she would feel strips of cold air exiting from the *Yongquan* point at the bottom of her feet, which is very comfortable. She insisted practicing morning and night. When schedule was tight, she would rise early and sleep late, doing basic exercises whenever time allows, and massages before going to bed. Only the 64 movements need to be practiced quietly for about 10 minutes. It's much cheaper and convenient than any retreat or spa! Hui Liu said, if practiced daily, it is quite easy to relax and meditate anytime to help recuperate both the body and the mind. Gradually, she can felt Qi moving among the organs, especially during meditation. For example, sometimes it's in the lung, then the large intestine. Just like what Chinese medicine said, lung and large intestine correspond to each other.

If I had a sore throat, I could feel a slight tickle at the sore spot, followed Qi movement in the lung or kidney. And the sore throat would be gone the 2nd day. These fine observations can only be felt during practice or meditation, which are evidence of Qigong in process of self-adjustment and healing the body.

My strongest and most interesting experience occurred when a mass of heat forms on my back while practicing the form. The mass grows bigger and hotter gradually. First about 2-3 inches wide, then 5-6 inches, always travels from the tailbone upward slowly. It felt very comfortable, but disappears when practice is done.

Another miracle appeared once during practice (at the standing meditation movement). An irresistible itch happened at the *Baihui* point. It had a diameter of a pencil and yet a mile long. Meanwhile, my whole body including my hands, arms, legs and feet felt clear and transparent as a crystal, a very pleasant feeling. I continued to practice until the end wondering why. Later I got an answer from Grandmaster Yang about this unique experience. She said, "Congratulations! That was Qi moving through the *xiao zhou tian*. The small *xiao zhou tian* means Ren and Du meridians are connected and are healthy. Big, *da zhou tian*, means all meridians are connected to Ren and Du meridians, and big change is about to happen physically." Truly, since the incidence, my body felt light and easy, like losing 30 pounds all the sudden, my head and thoughts are clear and much more energetic. Other improvements were:
1. Workload increased, but don't feel tired
2. Back pain & soreness disappeared. Back felt much stronger. Soreness in knees and finger joints also disappeared.
3. Don't get sick when others around me are sick, hardly cough anymore.
4. Menopause symptoms disappeared all at once.
5. Boost of confidence. With the help of black sesame seeds and green tea, my hair loss had stopped and teeth are stronger.
6. More cheerful, especially after practice every morning, feeling like a fully pumped ball with endless energy. People and things around appear more attractive and friendly, so is atmosphere at home.
7. More benevolent and generous since practice.
8. Became a vegetarian.

Dayan Qigong
About Master Hui Liu

9. Much healthier and younger, less wrinkles and spots on face.
10. Through the appreciation of Grandmaster Yang's teaching, I am pleased to follow the tradition and teach students about Dayan Qigong to the whole world.

I think these are the biggest benefits why monk Dao An invented Dayan Qigong, and Grandmaster Yang brought it to the public. This explains Hui Liu's reasoning for teaching Dayan Qigong with Grandmaster Yang's support to all of the students and instructors at Wen Wu School.

Dayan Qigong's sitting meditation is practiced with hands on the meridians points, plus mindless and selfless. It has great impacts on self-healing, development and restoring of the brainpower and stress release. Practice persistently every day, especially meditating before sleep to quiet the mind. Relax every cell in the body, use your own Qi to travel through the meridians to adjust and repair. When the brain is fully relaxed during mediation, it may feel like countless electrical wires moving and connecting in the brain. You'll hear music and charms you normally don't hear; seeing variation of colors, beautiful views and yourself with your eyes closed. All phenomena are natural, not to be alarmed or scared. But don't be overjoyed or pursuing it purposely. Just practice persistently (movements and meditation) 40 minutes every time, you'll experience these tranquilizing moments. Everyone will have a different experience, but it will be important for spiritual enlightenment. To all readers, continue practice for your own good!

Finally, words can't express my gratitude to many people who helped in completion of this book. First to Shari Chun, who took on a difficult task on photographing the pictures, editing and organizing the contents. She had spent countless nights and weekends. Thanks also to Loc Huynh for enhancing the photographs and assistance in all aspects. And to the many teachers and students for reviewing the book and their suggestions.

Thank you to my husband, Dr. Y.C. Chiang for the preface; my daughters, Dr. Erlene Chiang on medical information in the book, and Edith Chiang in translating the original articles from Chinese. To fellow Qigong practitioners and teachers, your comments are also welcome.

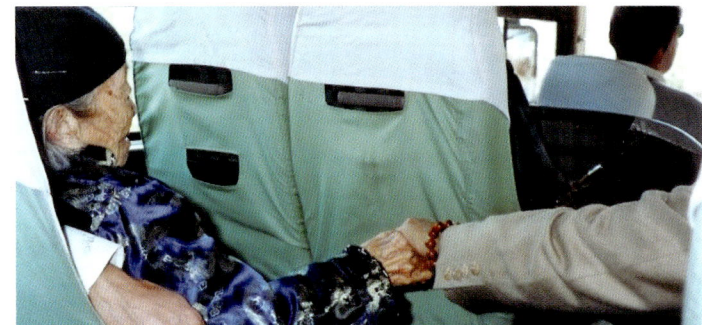

Grandmaster Yang and Master Hui Liu holding hands on the bus (2000)

Dayan Qigong
About Master Hui Liu

Sharing my experiences with many years of Dayan Qigong practice
By Hui Liu

One should be in a very peaceful, relaxed state when practicing Qigong. All the body parts, joints and the brain need to remain calm and relaxed. First, relax the hands and the back, and then slowly move up the neck and to the top of the head. Connect the *Baihui* point with the sky. After your shoulders are relaxed, check the elbows, wrist, *Laogong* points, the fingers and each joint of the fingers to the fingertips. Finally, check if the waist, pelvis, legs, knees, ankles and toes are relaxed. Keep your body relaxed and mind calm at all times during the practice.

Before you start the set, pause for a brief moment before beginning the form. By staying completely relaxed, Qi will run through all the body.

To be a human being is the most precious and appreciated thing in the world, so we need to make great efforts to keep learning, practicing, taking good care of our health, and staying active as well. And hence, we are able to study and cultivate our Qi. In order to practice Dayan Qigong, first keep the body relaxed and the mind calm. Focus on each movement. Only by doing this can one achieve the multiple goals through your practice. The feeling of Qi will get stronger as you practice. There are various feelings of Qi: heat, numbness, pain, itching, shaking, cold, tingling, swelling, expanding or shrinking. These are all natural sensations. These sensations are indications that Qi is flowing through and becoming strong inside the body. Let the feeling of Qi move, disappear, and stop naturally. Don't try to touch or lead the direction of Qi consciously. Qi moves vertically and/or horizontally sometimes, since Qi moves within the meridians. Everyone responds differently and some people have no particular sensations at all. Just follow what it is. Any disease can be cured, and one's health can improve when it is time.

It is important to keep the kidneys healthy. The kidneys are the first developed organs and affects blood production of the bones, bone marrow, reproductive system, intestines, lungs, ears and eyes. It is important to keep the kidneys warm by massaging the *Yongquan* and *Sanyinjiao* points frequently. Rub your hands until they are hot then place them on the lower back where the kidneys reside. Massage the kidneys up and down until you have a warm sensation in the back and throughout the body. Don't have sex too often. It is beneficial to eat black-colored foods. Keep the feet warm, especially if you live near the beach or in a place with high humidity or frequent rains. There are many movements good for the kidneys in Dayan Qigong. With healthy kidneys, a juvenile can improve his or her intelligence, learn faster, have good memory and develop a strong body; an adult can have a refreshed mind, focus on work and accomplish their goals; and a senior can prevent back pain, fatigue and memory loss.

It is desirable to avoid fried food, reduce consumption of salty, sweet and/or greasy food. One should have more fruits and vegetables of various colors. Do not overeat, and it is

Dayan Qigong
About Master Hui Liu

better to stop when you feel 80% full. Drink light and hot tea. Reduce the intake of raw and cold food.

Don't talk too much. Let the tongue touch the upper pallet just behind the front teeth. Think of your lower *Dantian* once in a while (but no need to focus on it) so there is a warm feeling. Before going to bed at night, keep calm and think about what you want to do the next day, or review the movements of Dayan Qigong in your mind or massage some pressure points and the lower *Dantian*. Stay in a Qigong mood day and night, as if you are meditating.

It is important to practice Dayan Qigong every day. Qi moves and directs blood circulating throughout one's body, for Qi is the leader of blood. Therefore Qigong should be done every day to promote Qi and meditate every day to cultivate Qi.

Wishes of good health and strong Qi for everyone.

Master Hui Liu with Qigong Master of 2004 Award

The 7th World Qigong Congress presenting to Master Hui Liu the Master Qigong for 2004 Award

Demonstrating Dayan Qigong at the 7th World Qigong Congress 2004

Dayan Qigong

Introduction

Four thousand years ago in ancient China, it is said, the legendary Yellow Emperor invented a technique of breathing and movement to vitalize mind and body. Records that describe breathing exercises exist from about 1,000 B.C. The Chinese, like the ancient Greeks, believed in a healthy mind in a healthy body, and discovered many techniques that were supposed to enhance health and well-being. It is not known exactly where or when Qigong[1] as we now know it began, but there have been many different styles that have evolved through the years.

1,700 years ago a venerable priest named Dao An developed a form of Qigong which he called Dayan Qigong. The Abbot Wan Yi then revised and perfected the set. Dayan Qigong was handed down from master to student as a secret or esoteric doctrine. Only in recent years that it's potential and benefits have become known to the general public, and is now widely taught in China.

"Da Yan" means "wild goose". In the Zhou Dynasty a wild goose was included in the wedding gift as a symbol of marital fidelity. In later times a wild goose was embroidered on the court robes of officials who had advanced in the civil examination system to the third highest level. The wild goose exemplifies high culture, and in ancient China it was not customary to kill them for food or game.

According to traditional Chinese thoughts, the wild goose embodies the Five Constant Virtues: "Ren" – ethics and perfect virtue free from selfishness; "Yi" – right conduct, loyalty and faithfulness; "Li" – respect, reverence, and good manners; "Zhi" – wisdom, knowledge, cleverness, and prudence; and "Xin" – truth and sincerity.

Wild geese migrate long distances, flying 1000 miles or more. They fly in a "V" formation, following naturally in a line. They always migrate on the same day to the same place. They mate for life. When a mate dies, the survivor laments, and it does not seek another mate. When the flock sleeps, they post sentries to warn of approaching danger. Although water birds, they are vegetarian. Thus, say the ancients, "to be a good person one must be like the wild goose."

In the 19th Century during the Qing Dynasty, Yang Mei Jun's grandfather learned Dayan Qigong from a monk. It was not until Grandmaster Yang's grandfather turned 70 that he decided to teach his granddaughter the form. Now Master Hui Liu is teaching the set here in the United States after she had learned the set from Yang Mei Jun.

Dayan Qigong
General Principles of Dayan Qigong

The Dayan Qigong set ("set" refers to the entire group of 64 movements) is based on the movements of the wild goose. It is structured in a way that enhances the circulation of Qi. "Qi" is a Chinese word whose concept is difficult to translate. "Qigong" literally means "Qi practice." Like the Sanskrit "Prana", the Japanese "Ki", and the ancient Greek "Pneuma," the word means both the vital life force and its existence.[1]

According to the Chinese theory of medicine, all illness is a result of obstructed Qi paths or an imbalance of yin and/or yang. Examples of yin are the dark, cold, inner, feminine, and negative force in the universe. Examples of the yang are the light, hot, outer, masculine, and positive force. Each contains within it the germ of the other. The two are combined in everything, and are inseparable from each other. Harmony is disrupted if the yin is too strong or if the yang is too strong, and vice versa.

Both Western physics and Eastern science describe the universe as a vast energy field. Dayan Qigong works to improve the various bodily functions by improving the body's electric and magnetic energy flow and capacity. The movements are organized to follow the flow of the earth's energy and to exchange internal Qi (from the body) and external Qi (from the earth, the universe), utilizing this energy to stimulate and balance the various functions of the body. Circulation of Qi can be governed by the mind. Concentration and relaxation are essential; therefore, to assure that Qi will flow strongly and without obstruction during practice. The movements combine the gentle and the vigorous, the soft and the hard in a systematic way to bring Qi to the blood, organs, bones, muscles, and ligaments as well as to the meridians, or channels, and the points. "Channels" are passages along which Qi and blood flow. On each channel are places where Qi is transported to the body surface, and these are the "points" used in acupressure and acupuncture.

Unlike other forms of Qigong, Dayan Qigong requires no special breathing techniques or mental images to facilitate the circulation of Qi. On a daily basis, practice in a relaxed state with the mind concentrated on the simple, graceful hand, leg, arm and body movements, will help the Qi flow through the channels, taking in the good Qi from the environment and expelling the sickness Qi from the body. For many of us whose lives are full of stress, complete relaxation may be a distant goal. It is nevertheless most important to concentrate on relaxation. The efforts of concentration will eventually increase your ability to relax. Additionally, it is very important not to do Dayan Qigong when you are angry, emotionally upset, or in a state of extreme agitation, or exhaustion. At such times the tension in the mind and body makes it impossible for the Qi to flow smoothly and naturally through the body channels.

---

1. "Like nature, Chinese words are alive and plastic, because thing and action are not formally separated." Ernest Fenollosa, *The Chinese Written Character as a Medium for Property*.

Dayan Qigong
General Principles of Dayan Qigong

Dayan Qigong is an effective exercise for the elderly. Within two months, elderly practitioners have experienced increased strength in the legs, improved muscle tone and joint flexibility, and overall vitality. Even the chronically ill, or people with physical disability can practice Dayan Qigong. It is especially helpful in treating disorders of the nervous system, the digestive system, the arterial and excretion systems, and osteoarthritis. The mentally ill can also benefit from practice, although it is important that they remain calm and physically capable during practice.

When practicing, wear loose and comfortable clothing. Clothes that are too tight will restrict the circulation of Qi. Do not do the set either immediately after eating or when you are extremely hungry. Wait at least 30 minutes after eating to begin and do not eat for 30 minutes after finishing. It is also best to move your bowels and urinate before starting. When doing the set, keep the body relaxed and natural, with the mouth closed. Gently place the tip of the tongue directly behind the front teeth on the upper palate.

While practicing Dayan Qigong, there may be a noticeable increase in the production of saliva. When saliva accumulates in the mouth, do not swallow it all at once. Instead, swallow it slowly in three parts, noticing its passage down into the stomach. This benefits digestion and directs Qi into the *Dantian*.

The *Dantian* is sometimes called the "Triple Heater" in English. It is not an organ, but rather three distinct areas on the body: in the forehead, middle of the chest, and in the abdomen below and behind the navel – where Qi can be stored. The primary function of Dayan Qigong is to store Qi in the *Dantian* to be able to control Qi and eventually generate Qi.

Scientific studies conducted in China have found that Dayan Qigong can have a therapeutic effect on hyper and hypo tension, weakness of the heart, insomnia, disturbances of the nervous system, intestinal infections, skin diseases, and mental illnesses. Scientific instruments have detected the presence of specific germs and viruses in the air around practitioners after they have expelled the sickness Qi from their bodies.

Dayan Qigong
Life Teachings of Grandmaster Yang Mei Jun

Introduction

Dayan Qigong is different from other forms of Qigong and martial arts, because it doesn't emphasize breathing techniques. Instead, it employs movements and thoughts to stimulate the human body's electromagnetic energy flow, known as Qi. For 1,700 Dayan Qigong was kept a secret internal marital art in the Taoist religion, handed down to carefully selected disciples. We are able to enjoy the benefits of Dayan Qigong thanks to the efforts of Grandmaster Yang Mei Jun, the 27th generation heir, and the students that she taught.

Grandmaster Yang Mei Jun passed away in July 2002, at the age of 108. Although she was short in stature, she was fast and agile. She was able to demonstrate extraordinary abilities: By directing her Qi she could appear as light as a feather or as heavy as a mountain. She could penetrate a wall with her Qi and check a person's illness without even seeing the person. She could produce five different fragrances from her palms. She could read words with her eyes closed, using only her yin tang (third eye) point. While practicing traditional Chinese sword, she could produce a ball of bright light at the tip of the sword, and could change the color of the blade of the stainless steel sword.

She used Qi to strengthen her health and to treat illness in herself and in others. She slept only 3-4 hours a night, and still maintained a radiant and youthful appearance. She practiced and taught without concern for money or power. Her profound and impenetrable power has attracted millions of people in the world. The walls of her house were covered with various plaques, prizes, awards, and well-deserved honors.

The Life of Yang Mei Jun

To understand this extraordinary woman, we should know something about her history and her life.

In the year of 1908, in the last dynasty of China, the Chinese were again in a period of civil war. Outside Xuan Wu Gate, in a quiet alley, lived a poor family of 3 generations. Then just 13 years old, Yang Mei Jun was the only grandchild in the Yang's family. Yang Mei Jun's grandfather, Yang De Shan was 73 years old. At age 73, he was still active and full of energy. His back was as straight as a pine tree. When he walked, the air stirred noticeably around his legs. One evening in mid-July, Master De Shan was bowing to the Buddha shrine in the house. He called his granddaughter, Yang Mei Jun in front of the Buddha and told her to kneel in front of the Buddha. Mei Jun had no idea what she did

Dayan Qigong
Life Teachings of Grandmaster Yang Mei Jun

wrong. Her eyes searched Grandfather's face for answers. When she saw that her Grandfather was not angry, her pounding heart gradually quieted down.

"Mei Jun, you are already 13 years old. There is something you should know about this family. I want to discuss something very important to you." Grandfather De Shan said, "When I was young, I was the only disciple of an old monk on the Kunlun Mountain. I lived with my teacher and learned the secret and spirit of Dayan Qigong. (DYQG) Before I left my teacher, I was told not to teach any student until I am 70 years old. I am now 73, and my son is 50 years old. If I teach my son, it is a little late." Therefore, after careful consideration, Grandfather De Shan decided to teach all he knew about DYQG to his granddaughter, Yang Mei Jun.

In the old days, there were many rules for accepting a student to study with you. Even though Mei Jun was his own granddaughter, she still needed to swear that she should never tell anyone about the learning experience of DYQG until she was 70 year old. She was not even to tell her own parents. Master De Shan told Mei Jun to move in with him in the back of the house, so they could practice Qigong in the middle of the night, when everyone else had fallen asleep.

The next day, early in the morning, Grandfather De Shan brought Mei Jun to the White Pagoda Temple. They walked for over an hour before reaching the temple. In front of the temple, there were a few vendors selling food and a few young men hanging around outside the temple. As they got closer to the temple, the vendors and the young people gathered around them. One of the young men reached out his hand trying to touch Mei Jun's face. But, before he could reach her face, Master De Shan scolded him by saying, "What do you think you are doing?" At the same time he pointed his left index finger at the young man's *Taiyang* point. At once, the young man loudly cried, "Ouch!" Then he fell back about 8 steps and sat down. His face was pale and gray. He could not speak or move. All the other people saw what had happened and opened a pathway for Master De Shan and Mei Jun.

Inside the temple, there were only a few visitors; there were tall incense burning, candles, and many Buddha statues. Master De Shan lighted some incense, and they both kneeled in front of the Buddha. Master De Shan read a few sentences silently to himself, and when he opened his eyes he told Mei Jun to look at the eight brass geese hanging on the wall. Then he said, "These wild geese are from the DYQG ancestors. Only the disciple from each generation knows about this secret, and where these geese are hanging. The physical positions of the 8 geese are some of the fundamental movements of DYQG. Mei Jun curiously stared at these 8 rusted geese. They were in different positions. One looked like it was flying high, one landing, and one flapping its wings. The number 7 goose had one leg forward; Mei Jun asked her grandfather, "What is this goose doing?" Master De Shan stated that this is one of the movements in Dayan palms exercise. The goose is fighting. This was, indeed, Mei Jun's first lesson of DYQG.

Dayan Qigong
Life Teachings of Grandmaster Yang Mei Jun

After they finished the ceremony they left the temple. On their way out, the loitering young men gave them a wide berth. Mei Jun asked her grandfather: "Grandfather, you were so wonderful. But how come all you had to do was point your finger at that man, and that stopped him?" Master De Shan replied, "I used my Qi to temporarily stop his circulation of Qi. Qi is the leader of blood. If Qi is congested, his head will be painful." Mei Jun said to her grandfather, "I am going to learn DYQG just like you." Master De Shan said that this is good. "But remember, practicing is for self-healing, self-defense, and healing of others. It is not meant for any other purposes." Mei Jun said, "healing others"? Master De Shan said, "Yes, we poor people do not have extra money to see doctors. So we have to rely on ourselves to regulate our Qi and blood to treat ourselves. Like myself, I am 73 years old. I am still very healthy. It is because I practice DYQG. Practicing Qigong is to practice the Jing, Qi, and Shen,"

JING: The body's most important essence that produces all fluids in the body, such as blood, sperm, body secretions, mucus, etc.

QI: Life force and vital energy that support all the body's function and functional uses of each system and organs.

SHEN: Spirit, spirit of oneself.

Grandmaster Yang stated: "If the Jing is full the Qi will be strong. If Qi is strong then Shen is abundant. If Shen is abundant, then the body is healthy, and a healthy body has less illness."

To avoid Mei Jun's parents and other people's suspicion, every midnight, Mei Jun followed her grandfather to practice in their yard. They never missed a day's practice. They began with the first set of DYQG. Although there are only 64 movements in the set, Mei Jun did not learn them easily. Her grandfather taught every movement 2 times without giving much verbal instruction. She learned every movement and their connection by quickly memorizing and carefully mimicking her grandfather. In the beginning, she was like all the beginning students, her back was sore and her legs were hurting, her whole body was tired. But she never stopped learning. It was very hard for a 13-year-old girl to wake up every morning between 3-5 A.M. to practice. Sometimes it was too hard for Mei Jun to wake up, so her grandfather kept encouraging her. He said, "You know why we practice between 3–5 A.M.? This is the time when Qi and blood run most abundantly. The lung controls the respiratory system and our Qi. This is the golden time to practice Qigong." After a while, the biological clock started to work, and Mei Jun woke up every morning at 3 A.M. to practice.

The cycles of the moon affect the ease of practice, but Mei Jun never became lazy in practicing. During the full moon, she felt that the effect of her practice doubled her energy. Her experienced grandfather never told her the connection of Qigong and a full moon. Mei Jun always thought there was a God living inside the moon, who watched her while

she was practicing and the God was helping her. It was not until years later that she realized the human's physiological body corresponds with the cycle of the moon. On a full moon day, the Qi and blood are more abundant, the muscles and internal secretions are stronger. Therefore, it is easier to practice. This was why she finished practice faster on a full moon day, but she kept practicing because she had committed herself to practice until 5 A.M.

After one year had passed, Mei Jun's movements were much better. They were like the wild goose's life: From dawn when the wild goose wakes up, shaking its wings, open its wings to flying, to look at the moon, searching for food and seeking a nest, every movement was perfect without any mistakes. Master De Shan was very satisfied with her granddaughter's performance. One night, shortly after one year of practicing, Master De Shan had Mei Jun sit in front of him and said, "let's celebrate our one year's hard work." Mei Jun was so happy. She thought to herself: "Great! After the celebration, Grandfather will teach me some new movements." But, instead of teaching her new movements, Grandfather started asking some boring questions about the first 64 movements.

Grandfather asked, "when we practice the first 64 movements, why are there more movements on the left side of the body than on the right? Why do many movements start with the left side of the body?" Mei Jun knew her Grandfather was testing her, so she said clearly, "many movements start from the left side of our body and to practice more on the left side of the body is one of the specialties of DYQG first set. Because the left side of the body belongs to blood and blood belongs to Yin. The right side of the body belongs to Qi and Qi belongs to Yang. Blood moves slower than Qi, Qi move faster than blood. To regulate and control the speed difference in the Qi and blood and to regulate the body's Qi and blood, we start on the left side of the body and do more movements on the left side."

Master De Shan was very proud of his Granddaughter's intelligence. He thought to himself, the Yang family is very proud to have such an offspring.

Master De Shan saw that Mei Jun had a strong foundation of Qigong, so he slowly taught her the second set, Dayan palm, Dayan sword, Dayan fist fighting, and others. At this time, Mei Jun's Qi was like the running river, everything seemed very easy to learn for her. She was able to master the movements and the philosophy quickly and easily. Like all other Qigong, DYQG is easy to learn; therefore students may think it is boring to learn. But, it never stopped Mei Jun from learning.

Ten years passed quickly. Civil war and war with Japan seemed like it would never stop. Life was getting harder each year. Mei Jun's grandfather and mother had passed away. In this poor family, there were only Mei Jun and her father left. Mei Jun's father was a taxi pulling man. He made his living by pulling people on a three-wheel cart. Mei Jun cooked and cleaned for her father. In these 10 years, she never skipped a day of practice. Even

Dayan Qigong
Life Teachings of Grandmaster Yang Mei Jun

though malaria killed many people at that time, she never fell ill. If she began to feel uncomfortable, she would practice Qigong to get rid of the evil Qi inside her body.

One evening, Mei Jun was waiting for her father to come home for dinner, but he never came back. She went out to look for her father, but could not find him. When she went back home, she saw a lot of people gathering inside their little house. Her father was covered with blood and unconscious. A Japanese soldier had stabbed her father after the soldier got out of the taxi and refused to pay. The last words her father said to Mei Jun were to go to Han Dan City to look for her aunt. Mei Jun was so angry that all she wanted to do was to seek revenge. Her neighbors stopped her from doing this, and told her she should go and look for her aunt. Dressed as a man, she buried her father, and then went in search of her aunt.

When Mei Jun arrived in Han Dan city, no one knew who her aunt was. It was still during wartime. Mei Jun could not imagine anymore what had happened to her aunt. Without a place to live, she joined a group that survived by selling salt.

Mei Jun continued to dress and act as if she were a man. Because of her years of practicing Qigong, she was very independent and strong. For many years, no one knew she was female. Later in the years of selling salt, she met a young man in the same group, with whom later she fell in love and married. His name was Chen Guo Ye. They lived a very poor life. Some Qigong masters used Qigong to heal others and had made good money for a living. But Mei Jun never forgot what her grandfather had told her. She continued to practice Qigong secretly at nighttime. Mei Jun's power grew with her continuous practice. She controlled her emotions, because her grandfather had told her over and over again, joy, anger, worry sadness, fear, depression, and fright are the cause of illnesses. So she always kept her thinking and emotions as peaceful as possible.

After she was married, she and her husband joined the army. They traveled a lot. Sometimes, going into the deep woods in the mountains, she met different Buddhist and Taoist monks and nuns. With them she studied and learned details of the body's meridians and points. These old monks and nuns had extraordinary power when meditating. Some nuns would lose track of time as they meditated, sitting for long hours. Some monks meditated in the freezing cold weather without extra clothing. Mei Jun benefited tremendously from discussions with them.

After Mei Jun and Guo Ye had settled down, one night Guo Ye woke up in the middle of the night and discovered his wife was missing. He sat up immediately to look for her. As he was approaching the door, he saw a black shadow lightly landing on the ground. The roof was about 10-11 feet high; this black shadow landed so lightly as if it was a feather. Guo Ye was going to call for help, but when he looked carefully, the black shadow was Mei Jun. Mei Jun was standing in the middle of their yard. She swung her arms up as if she was a wild goose flapping its wings; she then stood on her tiptoes, and jumped up to the roof. Then she quietly landed on the ground again.

Dayan Qigong
Life Teachings of Grandmaster Yang Mei Jun

"That was wonderful" Guo Ye said excitingly. "Mei Jun, I didn't know you knew martial arts, and you do it so well". Mei Jun told Guo Ye what she is practicing is called "Dayan Qigong". She told him that she had learned from her grandfather and she is the only heir of Dayan Qigong. Because she always practiced in the middle of the night and finished before he woke up, Guo Ye never knew about this. Mei Jun stated, "tonight, I knew you were about to wake up and I wanted to let you see what I can do, so you don't have to worry about us if the war continues and you have to leave us. I want you to know that I can take care of our son and myself.

The Chinese and Japanese war had finally stopped after 8 years, but Mei Jun had never stopped practicing. At age 60, she could project her Qi outward. Her third eye had been opened for years.

<u>The teachings become public</u>

In 1978, summer time, in the old forest of Xuan Wu park in Beijing, many observers surrounded a little old lady. This little old lady was a white haired, small sized woman. Mei Jun had treated many patients with her techniques by pointing at different points, slapping different areas, or by extending her five fingers over patient's body. Many people, hearing this, came from all over the place hoping Grandmaster Yang would also slap their body too!

One day, she sat on the grass and started talking. She said: "according to theories of Chinese medicine, Qi stagnation causes illness, but if Qi and blood are free flowing, then illness will disappear. The external Qi is a way for internal Qi to extend outward. Qigong practitioners that have strong Qi can send it out through their body parts, as a way to give treatments and a way to use the practitioner's Qi to treat others' illnesses. This is also the Qi that a Qigong master transforms his Qi in concentration form, to connect the sick area on the body, hence, to stimulate the patient's biological changes of the internal body, to increase its own immunity to fight against its own illnesses. I cannot treat all the people that come to ask me for 'slapping'. Because Qi is for storage purpose, it should not be expelled frequently. Every time I expel some of my Qi, I exhaust my own energy, if I exhaust too much, this old body cannot take it."

A middle aged man asked Grandmaster Yang, "Old master, it sounds like a mystery, but I am quite stubborn, I would like to see what "external Qi" looks alike, do you think it is "possible"?

Grandmaster Yang realized this is another great opportunity to advertise Dayan Qigong, so she told the crowd: "Look at that big tree over there, there is no wind in the air and the leaves on the tree is not moving at all. If I expel some Qi at the tree, let see what will happen to it?"

Dayan Qigong
Life Teachings of Grandmaster Yang Mei Jun

Grandmaster Yang moved her arms in the air a bit and pointed both palms at the tree, about 30 feet away. Suddenly, the leaves and branches began to move and sway. The crowd cheered and clapped.

Grandmaster Yang laughed and said: "This is a small trick that I just showed. After practicing Dayan Qigong for a while, everyone will be able to expel and send external Qi. If you practice longer and have stronger Qi, you can open your 'Heavenly eye', open your 'Heavenly door'. This is not a fantasy because it is doable. After practicing for a period of time, Qi will open this 'third eye'; this 'third eye' will be able to see things that normal eyes cannot see. If you also open *Tong Tian* point and *Baihui* point, then you opened your 'Heavenly Door', and you will be able to send signals to far away and pick up messages from far away."

In a half year, Grandmaster Yang gave Qi to various patients at different acupuncture points. She opened the blockages to their Qi and blood circulation. Over 100 people had regained their health. The words spread around quickly, very soon there was a rumor that there is a Goddess Yang that stays in the Xuan Wu park.

Grandmaster Yang got scared of her nickname; she did not like people to call her a goddess. She disappeared from the park and went to a remote hospital and started treating the patients with Qigong. Western medicine emphasizes on giving treatments, but it does not pay attention to the body's powerful own healing system. All effective treatments are just ways to bring healing, but the ultimate healing comes from the body's own healing system. Because our body has its own healing system, many people use exercises and not medicines to increase their own immune system to diminish illnesses. As Grandmaster Yang started to treat more people in the hospital, more people came to the hospital asking for her non-medicinal treatments. Some people even camped outside the hospital the night before to wait for her treatments. Even though she was treating many patients in the daytime, she still continued her practice. Sometimes she was tired, but she saw so many people recovered, she felt happy and peaceful. Instead of taking more sleep, she slept less but practiced more to start the next day's heavy workload with high energy.

One night the master could not fall asleep, she was thinking: "there are all kinds of Qigong that are being taught. It is very important to select the Qigong that is easy to grasp its meaning and is safe to learn. I am getting older, I want to start teaching this natural breathing technique Dayan Qigong exercise to the public to bring more benefits to people."

After working in the hospital for one year, making a large amount of money for the hospital, she resigned from the hospital. Instead she started teaching Qigong. In the park, she carefully selected 5 people to teach them Dayan Qigong. She wanted to start teaching them so they would then teach more students like in a snowball effect.

Dayan Qigong
Life Teachings of Grandmaster Yang Mei Jun

Grandmaster Yang's first group of students started practicing at 5 A.M. every morning under her strict supervision and guidance. To make a living, she continued to treat patients in the park for a very small fee.

One day she just arrived home from the park, a policeman came to her door and asked her to go the police station with him. Grandmaster Yang thought to herself, this is a bad sign. She collected her clothes and some food and was ready to follow the policeman to the station.

This policeman asked her: "Are you Madam Yang?"

Grandmaster Yang replied unwillingly: "If you already know then why are you asking?"

The policeman asked her: "I heard you are treating people, do you have a business license for operation? And how much money are you charging people?"

Grandmaster Yang replied: "I don't know".

Policeman said: "We already investigated that you are charging each person 30 cents".

Grandmaster Yang said: "What a good investigation".

Policeman asked again: "How do you treat people?"

"I point on people's head" Master said.

"Then wouldn't you kill people"? Policeman said.

"If I killed someone then I will pay back with my life. But I've treated over hundreds of people, I haven't killed anyone yet."

The policeman walked around Grandmaster Yang and said to her: "You are getting old, what kinds of illnesses can you treat"?

Grandmaster Yang began to feel impatient, and said to the policeman: "I can treat whatever illness you have."

The policeman thought for a while then said, "Our police chief has high blood pressure. We'll give you a chance and see what you can do!"

Grandmaster Yang came in front of chief and started to massage and gave Qi to the chief for a while. Suddenly the chief's red face and cloudy head became clear and his complexion became normal.

Dayan Qigong
Life Teachings of Grandmaster Yang Mei Jun

The Chief was very happy and said to Grandmaster Yang cheerfully: "You can go home now."

Grandmaster Yang pointed to her luggage next to her and said, "You want me to return home just because you wanted me to? I was ready to stay in prison."

The chief and the policeman were puzzled at her decision.

Grandmaster Yang then said "I was a pure and innocent person until you brought me in. You have to give me a certificate proving I am innocent and this certificate should act as an operating license for me to treat people in the future."

The chief was not willing to write such a certificate and Grandmaster Yang was not about to leave without it.

The chief finally relented and wrote a certificate that said Grandmaster Yang could treat people without disturbance from the police force in the future.

Her reputation spreads

When Grandmaster was 87 years old she became very famous because she treated a critical patient at the hospital that the doctors had pronounced dead.

While a police captain was on duty, his motorcycle hit a tree forcefully. He became unconscious immediately. His diagnosis was trauma to the brain, severe brain damage, facial bone fractures, and trauma to the internal organs. After staying in the hospital for 10 days, his condition got worse, he was having repetitive seizures, internal bleeding, pneumonia, severe loss of blood pressure, and a fever of 103°. On the 12th day, his urine showed protein and toxins. These were all signs of death. The hospital had alerted his family that his death was imminent.

The patient's son asked the primary doctor, Dr. Chang, Cun Zhong if he could bring Grandmaster Yang to treat him. With much hesitation, Dr. Chang finally agreed to it. He felt he had done everything he could for his patient.

Upon Grandmaster Yang's arrival, she looked at the patient. Then she asked Dr. Chang to remove all life support except glucose-infusion.

Dr. Chang knew once the life support was removed, the patient would die, but at the patient's son's request, he removed all the supports and stood quietly to see how Grandmaster Yang would treat this patient.

Grandmaster Yang waved her hands for a while and pointed her palms at the patient's *Renzhong* point and *Mingmen* point for a while. After 10 minutes, patient begun to spit

phlegm. After another 20 minutes, he began to excrete urine. After 2 hours, his blood pressure rose. He came out of the shock and coma condition. Dr. Chang was stunned at what he saw.

After that day, Grandmaster Yang came to the hospital daily to give Qi to the patient for ½ hour. On the third day, the patient's body temperature dropped down to 99°F. His pressure was steady at 110/70 mmHg; his white blood cell count went from 30,000 down to 10,000. On the 4th day, the patient gradually became conscious and he could respond by moving his legs. On the 5th day, patient held a conversation.

In a few more days, the patient's condition was back to normal and he was discharged from the hospital.

Dr. Chang convinced by Grandmaster Yang's fantastic healing power, begged the Grandmaster over and over again to take him as a student. Grandmaster Yang thought to herself, Chinese medicine doctors believed in energy flow in the meridians, but western doctors do not believe the energy flow. Maybe after Dr. Chang saw how she treated the untreatable patient, he changed his mind. Therefore she agreed and told him, "All right, you are a doctor of western medicine, we will pick a lucky day to have a ceremony for you to become my student." From then on, Dr. Chang was the first student of Grandmaster Yang from a western medical profession.

According to a famous biologist, Ba Fan, the human life span should be about average 125-150 years of age. There are two reasons why people can no longer reach this long life. First is caused from society from the stress level that lowers our immune system. Second is caused from nature. Illnesses come from "internal exhaustion", such as excessive sexual activities that exhaust our natural life force. According to Grandmaster Yang, Qigong practice requires calm, relaxation, quietness and at the same time limit sexual activities. This will reduce nervousness and stress both emotional and physically, also save one's natural life force. The results from practicing Dayan Qigong are proven by more people who practice this form. People came from all over China to listen to Master's speak and learn from the master. In 1979, Grandmaster Yang started the Dayan Qigong headquarter in Beijing China to accept students openly.

Throughout the next few years, she went from the Southern China to Northern China and from the Eastern to Western China. Sometimes people from the suburbs invited her to teach; Grandmaster Yang's students did not want to go because the pay was very small. Grandmaster Yang would say: "even the monetary return is little we will go anyway". In Kun Lun, China, because the living expense is very high, she lost money from teaching there, but when she saw Dayan Qigong study center was established in Kun Lun, she was very satisfied.

Dayan Qigong
Life Teachings of Grandmaster Yang Mei Jun

Everywhere Grandmaster Yang went, she spread the benefits of studying Dayan Qigong. She said: "People concentrate more on the external physical training exercises such as track and field, ball games and others skeletal and muscular exercises. People are unfamiliar with Qigong practice. Qigong is an exercise of the brain. Dayan Qigong trains and increases activities of the internal viscera and externally exercises on the physical body as well. Give Qi to the upper, middle and lower *Dantian*s and bringing nutrition to the whole body.

With each new class, she gained more fame and popularity. One day when she opened a class in Huang Shan (Yellow Mountain), all of the sudden the rain started. One of her students named "Da Zhou Yuen", which literally means big grassy field, was a famous wrestler in Mongolia. When Da Zhou Yuen saw rain dropped on the Grandmaster's head, he thought to himself. This skinny little old woman I can pick up two of them with my hands easily. How can I let the rain dropped on my teacher's head? So he ran towards his teacher and said: Teacher come to my back, I will carry you." Grandmaster Yang did not reject his invitation and she climbed on his back. Immediately he felt as though there were 1,000 pounds of weight on his back. His legs shook, and he couldn't take a step. Grandmaster Yang said to Da Zhou Yuen: "What's the matter with you my big student? It's raining so hard, why aren't you going?"

Da Zhou Yuen put the Grandmaster down on the ground and bowed to his teacher. He then said: "Grandmaster, I am sorry for my clumsiness, I will never do this to you again. I will be your student forever!"

In Hong Zhou State, there were two more mysterious stories that enhanced Grandmaster Yang's fame. There was a Marine Sergeant about 50 years old. He had an operation in the anus area for a lesion, and the lesion did not close. For a long time he could not sit down or lie flat on his back. He could only lie on his stomach when he slept. He heard that Grandmaster Yang was teaching nearby, so he stood outside the classroom and learned by listening from the outside. He practiced for two weeks and his lesion closed completely. Another story involved a different soldier. For over 20 years he suffered from low back pain and he could not bend his back. He learned the first 64 movements for ten days, one day as he was practicing a movement named "Rinse Waist", he heard a sudden cracking sound from his back. He screamed loudly, "I can bend my back now!" His classmates congratulated him for his improvement as they saw this soldier bend his back and reach down to his knees.

Movement and Thought

Many people think that practicing Qigong should be combined with special thoughts as they practice. It seems like special thoughts will bring them special Qi effects and power. But Grandmaster Yang emphasized practicing Dayan Qigong without adding special thoughts and breathing techniques. Dayan Qigong uses movements to increase the body's internal Qi circulation, open any blockages in the meridians and the points, increase

Dayan Qigong
Life Teachings of Grandmaster Yang Mei Jun

blood flow to decrease stagnation, and increase the body's metabolic and immune system functioning.

Relaxation

Grandmaster Yang said "Regulate and balance the mind to reach quietness stage". This is fundamental for successful Qigong practice. "Relaxation" should start from the waist. When the waist is loose and relaxed, then the whole body can relax naturally. For beginners who feel cold and soreness, which means the movements are too stiff and the body is not relaxed. If the palms are hot like fire burning, hands and feet are warm, that means the body is fully relaxed and the blood is concentrated in certain areas of the body. Grandmaster Yang said Confucius once said: "Keep your eyes straight without looking at evil." This is a good way to describe Qigong practice. When we are practicing, if we can stop our wondering mind, then our Qigong practice will improve tremendously.

Grandmaster Yang also said: "Beginners should always be in the relaxed and quiet stage while practicing." When the body is under such quietness stage, movements will occur. For instance, some may have involuntary physical movements of all kinds that the body moves by itself. In Dayan Qigong practice, there is usually no such phenomena as described above. Therefore Dayan Qigong is safe to practice. But as your Qi becomes stronger by itself, you can see fire like types of Qi expelling from fingertips. Some people with stronger Qi can have Qi as long as a few meters. If Qi is condensed, you will see halo or aura types of lights as in Buddha, sometimes there are lights shining on the hands as bright as the stars.

Balancing Yin and Yang

Grandmaster Yang advised, "Before practicing, you should be able to differentiate what are the Yin and Yang and what is *Dantian*". Our body's upper body is Yang and lower body is Yin. Our back is Yang and front is Yin. The right side of our body is Yang and the left side is Yin. Lower *Dantian* is located in the abdomen, it is also known as "Qi Hai" which literally means sea of Qi. At this location, the Qi and blood is concentrated. This is the place where men store sperm and women nurture babies. The body's life force relies on "original Qi" or the "Yuen Qi". In the first set, twenty-one movements give Qi directly to the lower *Dantian*, where the Yuen Qi is stored. The middle *Dantian* is located in the *Tanzhong* point in the middle of the chest, between the two nipples. Middle *Dantian* is also the connecting point where the upper and lower *Dantian* meets and where all the meridians' Qi connect at this point. It dominates the body's "Zhong Qi" or the afterbirth Qi and where nutrition is stored. In Dayan Qigong movements, many movements give Qi to the middle *Dantian* to give nutrient to the heart and lungs' system. The upper *Dantian* is also the *Yintang* point. *Yintang* point is located between the two eyebrows. In the area surround *Yintang* point, this is the area as the central support of all the meridians, the fountain of intelligence, where it stores the person's "Shen Qi" or the "Spiritual Qi". Dayan Qigong's first set makes more practice on the upper *Dantian*. About 20% of the first 64

Dayan Qigong
Life Teachings of Grandmaster Yang Mei Jun

movements increase the functions of the upper *Dantian*. The upper *Dantian* increases the brain's functions and intelligence, enhances the nerves and the body's fluids' regulatory system, and improves the body's self- healing system. To make more practice of the upper *Dantian* also treats anemia in the brain, low blood pressure, headaches, lack of Qi and blood in the brain, "sunken Qi" and prolapsed Qi.

<u>Proper Stance</u>

"Two feet stand parallel at the shoulders' width is the basic foot step of Dayan Qigong". Standing like this balances the three Yin and three Yang meridians of the foot as well as balance our posture, as we stand straight. Open the five fingers naturally, keep the thumb and index finger open or keep the "tiger's mouth"[1] open is the basic hand shape of Dayan Qigong. In general, try to keep the back of your hands in the same plane as the back of your forearms. This opens the wrist and fingers and is referred to as "Beautiful Ladies' wrists." This brings more Qi circulation to the hands three Yin and the three Yang meridians to finger tips, so Qi and blood will have better circulation in the hands. "Mouth slightly closed. Tongue touching the upper pallet just behind the teeth" is another basic requirement of Dayan Qigong. This helps connect the Du (Governor) vessel and the Ren (Conception) vessel, to increase internal Qi circulation. While the tongue is in this position, the saliva that is produced is better for digestion and prevents aging.

"You must also remember, during practice and five minutes after practices do not open your mouth, this will consolidate the heaven and earth Qi you've received during practice." I see many Qigong practitioners in the park, they always talk while they are practicing or laughing during their practicing, and they are just wasting their hard work.

As Grandmaster Yang walked and looked around her students, she saw a female student practicing quietly in the corner. She shouted at the woman: "What are you doing?"

The female student did not understand what was going on? Grandmaster Yang asked again: "Is this how my students taught you?" The female student opened her eyes widely still puzzled by the Grandmaster.

Grandmaster Yang called one of her teaching assistant over and said: "Kim, come here! You tell me what is wrong with her practice?"

Kim said easily: "She should not be practicing nearby the open sewer." "Qigong is a breathing exercise, it also expels the body's evil Qi, accepts good Qi from the heaven and earth. Therefore never practice nearby a polluted area."

Grandmaster Yang said: "You are only half right. Take another look at this student and tell me if she is practicing towards the right direction?"

33

Dayan Qigong
Life Teachings of Grandmaster Yang Mei Jun

Now everyone understood the problem, because this student was practicing facing the West.

"As you all know, how you place the radio will interfere with its signal reception. Practicing Qigong is the same thing. Our face should be facing the East or the South. The east is the direction from which the sun rises, symbolizing growth and provides stronger Qi. The South, according to Chinese geomancy (*Feng Shui*), is an auspicious direction symbolizing movement, light, fire, and the heart."

A student stated to Grandmaster Yang that they saw and smelled the fragrant Grandmaster Yang was expelling and wondered if she can explain what it was. Grandmaster Yang replied, "You thought I was using perfumes right? She said in the natural world, there is fragrance in every living thing, especially plants and animals. Their smell can be felt and smelled by humans easily. If you put your hands in front of a very fragrant flower for a while, you will smell its fragrance on your palm. If you practice nearby pine and cypress trees, your body will have such smell too. People who practice in floral gardens will have floral fragrance. Fragrance can store inside our body and can be expelled whenever we want to. Grandmaster Yang also said, I have stored for over 70 years of fragrance inside my body, I was just letting it out a little bit, what is the big deal?"

Qigong and Illness

A survey done by ten Dayan Qigong study centers showed that about 71% of students suffered chronic illnesses. After practicing for 1 to 3 months, 95% of their illnesses were noticeably improved. The frequency and severity of their symptoms had decreased. Students with neurasthenia and digestive system diseases were cured. Students with heart diseases, hepatitis, or chronic nephritis after practicing for 6 months to one year, about 90% or above students had their health returned to normal.

Grandmaster Yang successfully treated many cancer patients in ten years. She said human's diseases about 50-80% of times are caused by emotional stress. When a person reaches relaxation and quietness stage while practicing Qigong, the body will not be disturbed with unhealthy signals either from inside or outside of the body. Once a cancer patient controls his own emotion, signs of cancer can disappear. If the cancer patient can receive Qigong treatments at the same time, the external Qi can move through various acupuncture points on the patient while joining with patient's own Qi, this will increase and induce patient's own immune system to kill cancer cells so the body can return to its original equilibrium status.

In the late 70's, scientists in China found that the Qi that comes out of a Qigong master's palms is similar to low frequency (4 to 10 cycles/sec) electromagnetic waves. These waves are likened to a mother's patting her baby's back to comfort the child, the rocking of a crib, light music, or the lapping of water hitting a rock in the ocean. Their studies showed Qigong treatment is same as giving a low frequency sonic stimulation, and induces a

relaxed and quiet stage in the recipient. In 1987, volume 23, "*Half Moon Magazine*", the Marine hospital showed that sending or expelling Qi sends infrared waves, electrical waves, and sound waves. These are all cancer-killing agents. A Qigong treatment on cancer patient for 60 minutes can kill cervical cancer cells up to 59.6%. Similar treatments for stomach cancer patient resulted in the death of up to 25% of the cancer cells. If cancer patients can practice Dayan Qigong consistently then there will be constant improvement.

The spread of Qigong

In the ancient martial arts world, martial arts techniques and practice have always been kept secret from the outside world. Before Grandmaster Yang, Dayan Qigong could only be revealed to one student after 70 years of age. Grandmaster Yang was the first person that changed the secretive world. In ten years, she had 400-500 acknowledged students. Now there are between five to six million students throughout China, Hong Kong, Australia, Singapore, United States of America, New Zealand, Malaysia, Philippine, Japan, Sweden, Germany, Canada and etc. Many of these students have immense

Qigong power. Some can give Qigong treatments, some can feel illnesses with their hands, some can send messages and some have x-ray vision with their eyes.

Grandmaster Yang always encouraged her students to practice more and more Qigong. She used herself as an example that she practiced hours after hours without resting in any kinds of weather and without any excuses for not practicing. She said many scientists believe that humans have extra-ordinary potentials that come out in special conditions. There are documented instances of slightly built women lifting an automobile to rescue their trapped child. These extra-ordinary powers can be fully exposed under special circumstance but can also be trained with Qigong. The human brain has about 140 billion brain cells. After 60 years of age, the brain cells begin to die about 100,000 cells per day. After certain amounts of cells are diminished, the human will die. Therefore to have longevity, we have to bring to an end to the death of brain cells. Practicing Dayan Qigong decreases secretion of growth hormones, and slows down metabolism of protein. Because the exhaustion of the brain cells and nerves are less consumed, this elongates the brain and nerve cells' life spin.

Grandmaster Yang was also very generous to her students. Everywhere she started a study center, she paid for all of the expenses. Her magnetic power attracted many fellow students from all over China. In the hot summer time, she bought the mosquito nets for all the students. In the cold winter, she bought clothes for those students who did not have enough clothes.

Dayan Qigong
Life Teachings of Grandmaster Yang Mei Jun

There was one time on the way to start a new study center that her students did not listen to her advice. They were treating people on their way to their next destination. The trip was rough and the students were sick from giving treatments to too many patients. Grandmaster Yang was very upset; she had those students to line up in front of her. She said: "I told you many times not to teach Qigong and treat patients at the same time. You never listened. All you think about is how much money you can make from it. Why don't you realize if you teach many people Qigong you can have more influence on them about taking care of their own health. Instead of treating a few people here and there! I told you if your foundation of Qigong and your Qi is not yet strong, you should not give Qi frequently like you are doing, this is harmful to your health and destroy the benefit of practicing Dayan Qigong. I am not fooling you; you have to know Qigong masters can receive good Qi from the external environment to benefit themselves. They can also receive sickness Qi. If you are surrounded by sickness Qi all the time, after a while, these sickness Qi can penetrate through your meridians and acupuncture points that will cause illness to your organs and you will be ill too. Many people that have sensitive meridians are ill because they are often surrounded by sickness Qi, evil and dirty Qi. After a while, they become weak and ill. Teaching Qigong exhaust your energy already, if you teach and treat at the same time, you are exhausting lots of your own energy. How can your body take this kind of abuse? I can't believe how you treat my words like trash. I also know that you are spreading words about me that you've said Grandmaster Yang is old-fashioned with old thinking. She doesn't understand about business, there are a lot of businesses out there and she doesn't let us make money. Grandmaster Yang's students saw their teacher was angry, they felt ashamed.

Grandmaster Yang continued by saying: "After careful consideration, if you don't correct your acts, we should split up to our own way. You can teach Qigong, treat people, make more money, and I don't care. But just remember never use my name as advertisement for your business."

Grandmaster Yang's high quality of character and behavior influenced all her students. When she started a study center, she never charged a lot of money. When she gave treatments, if the patient couldn't pay her, she thought to herself this is just another way to spread benefits of Dayan Qigong. She never bluffed about her power and treating ability. She always told her patients that besides receiving Qigong treatments, they should also go to the hospital for further check-ups. She told students the best Qigong is the kind that can treat illness and bring good health.

When Grandmaster Yang heard that over 10,000 students are practicing Dayan Qigong in a park in Yunnan province, in the city of Da Li, she was very happy. What made her even more excited was hearing that thousands of students in the United Sates were practicing Dayan Qigong. This powerful but gentle form is based on the movements of the wild goose. In a sense, all the students practicing today are the heirs and children (or "goslings") of Grandmaster Yang.

Dayan Qigong
Life Teachings of Grandmaster Yang Mei Jun

In 1998, Dayan Qigong was selected by Chinese government Department of Physical Education for its safety and effectiveness in both therapeutic purposes and completeness in both physical form and meditation form.

Grandmaster Yang passed away in 2002. Her teaching lives on.

Students practicing in Berkeley, California.

Dayan Qigong
Life Teachings of Grandmaster Yang Mei Jun

道德得道正道行

When personal virtue is valued, the right Tao will flourish.

Grandmaster Yang meditating

Grandmaster Yang Mei Jun practicing at 80 years old

Dayan Qigong
Life Teachings of Grandmaster Yang Mei Jun

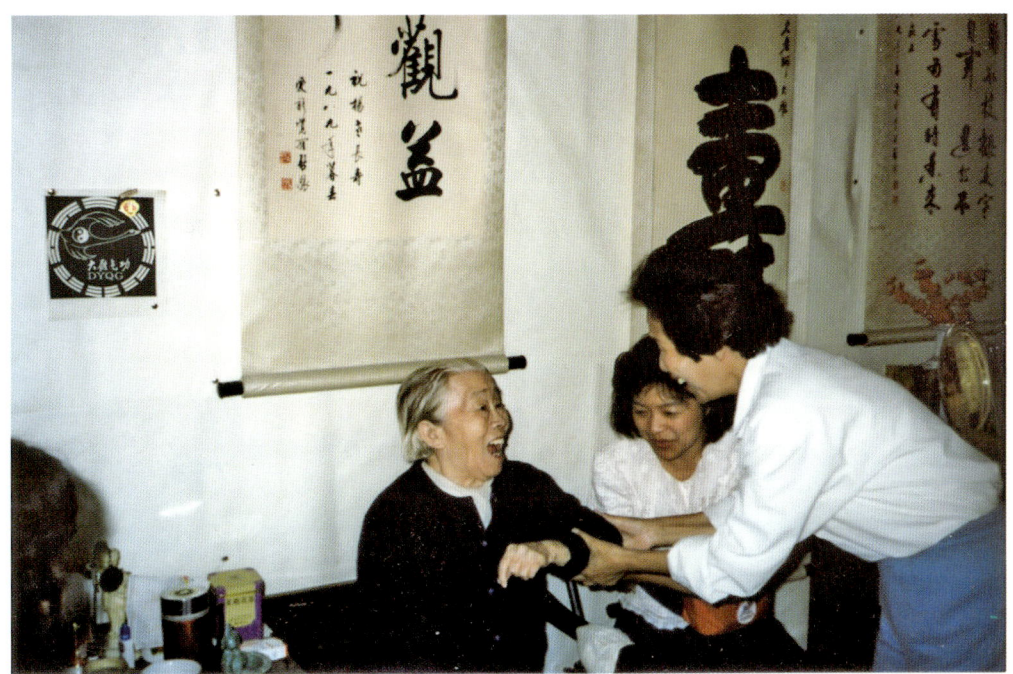

Here are two people trying to lower Grandmaster Yang's arm and cannot do it.
She is very happy and strong.

Toasting to Grandmaster Yang during lunch

Dayan Qigong
Life Teachings of Grandmaster Yang Mei Jun

Grandmaster Yang demonstrating qigong during lunch

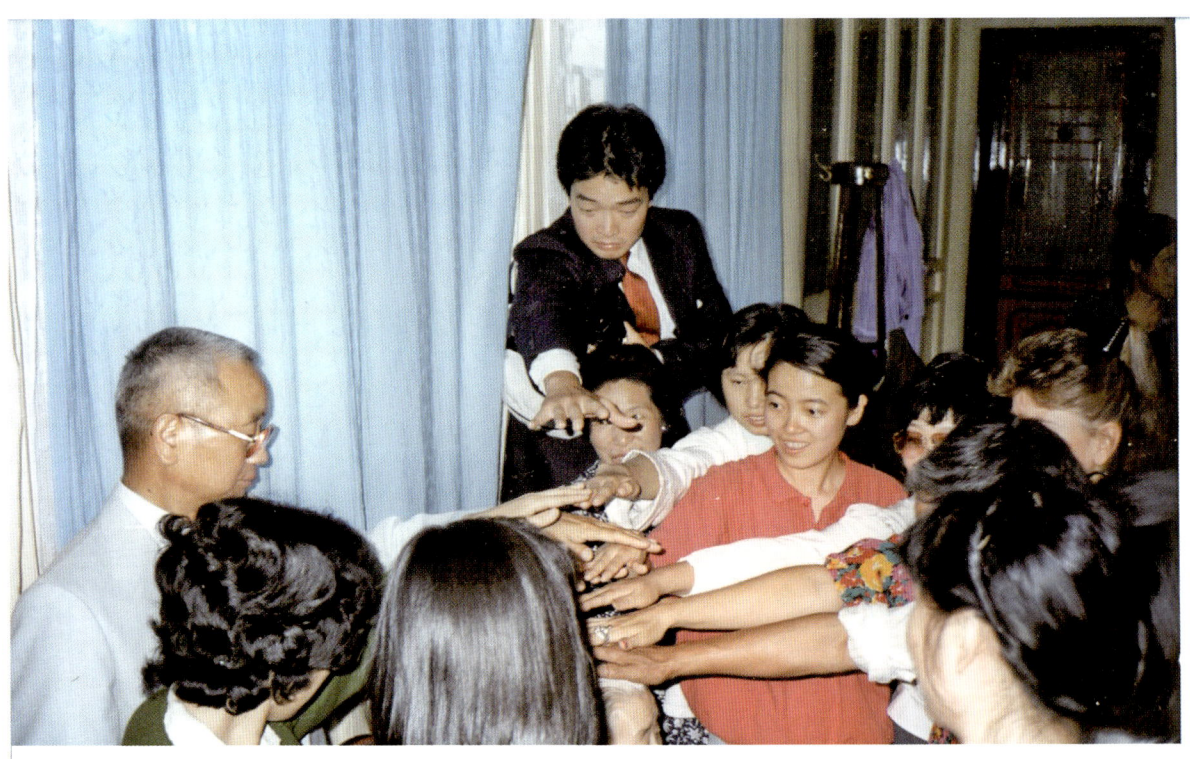

Feeling Qi emitting from Grandmaster Yang's *Baihui* point

Dayan Qigong
Life Teachings of Grandmaster Yang Mei Jun

Demonstrating Qigong in the park

Dayan Qigong
Life Teachings of Grandmaster Yang Mei Jun

Dr. Erlene Chiang, Grandmaster Yang, and Master Hui Liu doing meditation

Grandmaster Yang practicing in the park

Dayan Qigong
Life Teachings of Grandmaster Yang Mei Jun

Grandmaster Yang, Master Liu and Grandmaster Sun (Taiji Master, far right in front) walking in the park

Master Hui Liu with Grandmaster Yang

Dayan Qigong
Basic Warm Ups and Massage

1. Waist Rotations 揉腰

1-1

Stand straight naturally with feet together, eyes looking forward and afar. Close the mouth with the lips lightly touching and the tip of the tongue lightly touching the upper palette just behind the front teeth. Keep breathing naturally and the whole body is relaxed (1-1).

Clockwise rotation: Place the hands on both sides of the waist with the thumbs pointing forward toward the abdomen and the other fingers resting on the kidneys. Use waist as the "axis point" and rotate in a clockwise circle for 20 times. Try to keep the head stationary.

1-2

Massage the kidney using an up and down motion for 10 times, and then massage crosswise for 10 times (1-2).

Counterclockwise rotation: Repeat the rotations in the counterclockwise direction for 20 times.

Massage Middle *Dantian* (Zhong *Dantian*)

Place the both hands on the chest in the middle, with the left hand on top. Massage the area by making a circle to the left around the chest area for 10 times. Then, switch hands so the left hand is on the bottom, and massage making circles around the chest area to the right 10 times (1-3).

1-3

Functions:
This exercise is like giving gentle massage to the spleen, stomach, liver, lungs, small intestine, large intestine, urinary bladder, and the reproductive systems. When the hands are placed on the kidneys, the "Qi" is provided to the kidneys. The rotation brings gentle rubbing movements between each vertebra; therefore, spinal and back problems can be prevented. This movement also reduces fat deposits in the waist region. The ankles are rotating at the same time to increase strength and flexibility of the ankles and consequently to reduce the possibility of ankle injuries.

Dayan Qigong
Basic Warm Ups and Massage

2. Hip Rotations 揉胯

2-1

Clockwise rotation: Stand straight, naturally (whole body relaxed), feet parallel, shoulders' width apart. Place hands on hips across pelvic bone, the thumbs open pointing forward toward the abdomen, the other fingers of the hands on the *Huantiao* point (GB 30). Rotate in large circles 20 times clockwise (2-1).

Massage *Huantiao* and Lower Sacral Area

Huantiao (GB 30) is located on the Gallbladder Meridian in the dimple of the buttocks, near joint of the hip. The point is very deep. See *Huantiao* point on (2-2).

2-2

Massage the *Huantiao* points by pressing the fingers on the *Huantiao* points and quickly rotate the fingers 10 times. Massaging this point helps to relieve pain in the lumbar region and thigh.

Massage the lower back by placing the hands on the back and rub up and down 10 times. Massage the lower back improves the urinary bladder function.

Counterclockwise rotation: Repeat the hip rotations 20 times counterclockwise.

Massage the Lower *Dantian*

2-3

The lower *Dantian* is located one-half inch deep, behind the navel. This is the fountain of original Qi.

Place the right hand over the navel and the left hand on top. Massage in a circle around the navel to the left for 10 times, then, switch hands so the left hand is on the bottom and over the navel, right hand on top, and massage around the navel to the right 10 times (2-3).

This massages the organs and meridians around the lower stomach.

Functions:
This movement is for exercising and massaging the large intestines and small intestines, the reproductive and excretory systems, and the tendons and bones near the pelvis, and the sciatic nerve. The *Huantiao* point (GB 30) is an acupuncture point on the Gallbladder

Dayan Qigong
Basic Warm Ups and Massage

Meridian. Stimulating it will strengthen the back and the legs. Placing the fingers on the *Huantiao* point will both increase its functions and provide Qi to the point. The bottoms of the feet are also massaged with the rotation of the hip.

3. Knee Rotations 揉膝

3-1

3-2

Place the feet together, bend forward, back straight and relaxed, while squatting down slowly, rest the hands lightly on the knees. Eyes looking forward, keeping both knees together, rotate the knees 10 times in a clockwise direction (3-1).

Then, with the hands still on the knees, straighten the legs and massage the knees in circular motions 10 times (3-2). Maintain good body balance at all times.

Repeat the rotations 10 times in counterclockwise direction. Massage the knees in a circular motion 10 times in the opposite direction as above.

Now, squat down even lower and lift both heels. Keeping the knees together, rotate them clockwise 10 times.

Keeping the legs straight, massage the legs from the *Huantiao* down to the angles on the outer legs 10 times.

Repeat the deeper knee rotation counterclockwise 10 times, and massage the inside of the legs from the ankles up to the groin 10 times (in the direction of the meridian).

Functions:
This movement exercises the elasticity of the ligaments in the knees and strengthens the ankles for preventing difficulty in walking and stiff legs. It is also good for treating and preventing arthritis in the knees and ankles. Frequent practice of this movement will maintain walking ability.

Dayan Qigong
Basic Warm Ups and Massage

4. Four Movements: (a) Circular Push, (b) Back Bend, (c) Side Stretch, and (d) Forward and Side Bends (四個動作)

4-a1

4-a2

(a) Circular Push 前轉圈:
Put the legs together and keep them straight. Interlace the fingers of both hands, thumbs touching each other at the tips, open the palms, and push palms outward. Push hands out to the front (4-a1), up, and then downward close to the body. Push both hands out in a circular direction from the front to above the head (4-a2) and then down along the front of the body to the abdomen. Start pushing to the front again and repeat. Do this for 20 circles.

(b) Back Bend 後翻:

4-b1

Raise both arms to the sky with 10 fingers interlaced and palms facing to sky (4-b1). Then bend back by stretching the spine as far as possible and still feeling comfortable. Bring back to the standing position. Do this 5 times.

(c)

4-c1

4-c2

(c) Side Stretch 側伸(右)(左):

Raise both arms to the sky, fingers interlaced with palms facing the sky. Stretch to the right side of the body (4-c1), and then straighten up. Do this for 5 times. Then stretch to the left side of the body (4-c2), and then straighten up. Do this for 5 times.

Dayan Qigong
Basic Warm Ups and Massage

(d) Forward and Side Bends 前折下按（中，右，左）:

4-d1

With fingers interlaced, bend down forward at the waist and press the palms to the ground (4-d1), keeping the knees straight. Lift up the head so the *Baihui* point (Du 20 or GV 20) is pointing forward. Make a circle each time by stretching downward, forward, upward, and finally downward. Repeat 20 times. Then, stretch both arms straight down in front to the ground down and up for 5 times. After 5 times, turn the upper body 90° to the right and push the palms down to the right side of the foot 5 times. Then turn body to the left side of the foot and push down and up for 5 times.

Functions:

This series of movements exercises the fingers, wrists, elbows, shoulders, back, and the lateral sides of the ribs. They are good for preventing arthritis and degeneration of the joints. Also, stretching downward relaxes the tendons and bones of the lower body and the legs.

5. Forward Bend 前折: Elbow to Ankle 肘到腳踝

5-1

Forward Bend, Elbow to Ankle 前折, 肘到腳踝:
Legs are straight and feet together. Cross both arms by holding the elbows in front of the chest. Bend the waist forward, hold the elbows, and push down towards the ground, outward, upward, and finally inward. Lift up the head so the *Baihui* point is pointing forward. Push in a circle for 10 times (5-1).

Bend forward, legs are straight and together, hold the elbows with each hand and push down 5 times.

5-2

Massage the legs by rubbing the outsides of the legs starting at the *Huantiao* to the ankles for 5 times. Then slap the outside of the legs from the *Huantiao* to the ankles for 5 times. Try to keep the back straight and relaxed (5-2).

Dayan Qigong
Basic Warm Ups and Massage

6. Head to the Toe 頭到腳

(a) Shallow Stretch:

6-a1

Extend the right leg about 1~2 feet out front at 45° angle and flex the right toes upward. Keep the right leg straight and bend the left leg. Left hand holds the right elbow and the right hand hold the left elbow. Bend at the waist and make small, shallow circles with the forearms over the top of the ankles for 10 times (6-a1). Keep the body centered and balanced at all times.

6-a2

While stretching, lower the body only as far as comfortable.

Then place 10 fingers on the ground on each side of the foot. Stretch down 10 times by bending at the waist (6-a2). The back should remain straight while bending down. The *Baihui* point should point forward.

6-a3

With the body still bent forward, massage the leg by rubbing down the extended leg starting from the *Huantiao* point on the outside and the groin on the inside, down to the ankle, and then reverse direction and rub upwards. Press harder on the outside going down and harder on the inside coming up for 5 times (6-a3). Then slap the legs in the downward direction only from the *Huantiao*/groin to the ankle, harder on the outside of the leg and lighter on the inside. Do this for 5 times.

Repeat the stretching on the left leg. Massage and slap leg.

Functions:

This exercise helps to relax the joints and the muscles, increase circulation to the legs, and prevent aging and stiffening of the tendons and the bones.

Dayan Qigong
Basic Warm Ups and Massage

(b) Deep Stretches:

6-b1

6-b2

Place 3 fingers on the ground on each side of the foot, using the thumbs, index and middle fingers. Stretch down 10 times by bending at the waist (6-b1). The back should remain straight while bending down. The *Baihui* point should point forward. Repeat again with only the 2 index fingers on the ground (6-b2).

6-b3

Then try to grab the right foot with the hands (keep right leg straight). Bend the upper body forward and try to touch the tip of the foot with the forehead. Try this 10 times (6-b3). Massage and slap leg.

Now try to stretch even lower and make 10 deep stretches.

This is an advanced warm up exercise. Do it carefully, and at your own limitations

6-b4

With the body still bent forward, massage the leg by rubbing down the extended leg starting from the *Huantiao* point on the outside and the groin on the inside, down to the ankle, and then reverse direction and rub upwards. Press harder on the outside going down and harder on the inside coming up for 5 times (6-b4). Then slap the legs in the downward direction only from the *Huantiao*/groin to the ankle, harder on the outside of the leg and lighter on the inside. Do this for 5 times.

Repeat the stretching with the left leg straight to the front. Massage and slap leg.

Functions:

This exercise is for stretching the tendons and the ligaments in the back of the legs to help them stay long and flexible. Prolonged practice of this movement helps improve walking balance and can keep the body stay young. Practicing this exercise is also very important and fundamental to one's success in martial arts.

Dayan Qigong
Basic Warm Ups and Massage

7. Standing Heel and Toe Kicks 踢腿

7-a1

(a) Heel Kicks 蹬腳:

7-a2

Stand with the feet parallel to the shoulders. Place the hands on the waist with thumbs pointing forward and the rest of the fingers on either side of the kidney. Flex the right foot upward and kick diagonally toward the left side of the body in a 45° position. When kicking, lift the right knee and use the strength from the knee to kick the heel out. Bring the leg back on ground. Do the same for the left, and kick diagonally towards the right. Kick alternately to each side 10 times.

7-b1

For beginners, start with low kicks (7-a1); then as practice advances, kick higher (7-a2).

(b) Toe Kicks 腳尖踢腿:
Stand and place the hands as in the heel kicks. Point the right toes and kick diagonally towards the left (7-b1). Lift the right knee and use the strength from the knee to kick the toe out

Bring the leg back on the ground. Do the same for the left leg, and kick diagonally towards the right side. Kick alternately to each side 10 times.

Start with low kicks; then as practice advances, kick higher (7-b1).

8. Turn Neck Stretches (Grasp Ear) 頸部扭轉

8-1

Put the right hand on left shoulder. Push the right elbow upward with the inside of the left elbow. Then turn head to the right and try to grab the right ear with the right fingers. The left palm faces the left ear (8-1). Stay for 10 seconds. Put both arms down to relax.

Repeat on the opposite side (8-2). Do both sides two times.

8-2

Dayan Qigong
Basic Warm Ups and Massage

Functions:

This exercise stretches the shoulder and the back. When the neck turns, the muscles and the bones are relaxed and stretched. This can help prevent blockage of Qi and blood in the head and the neck region, alleviate neck and shoulder pain, treat high blood pressure, and prevent hardening of the blood vessels, and benefits the many meridians that passes through the neck.

9. Slap Shoulder and Under Arm 肩部和腋下拍打

9-1

Stand with the feet together and the legs straight. Stretch out both arms to the sides of the body, palms facing out (forward) and arms at about shoulder height. Cross both arms so the right hand slaps the left shoulder *Jianyu* point (LI 15) and the left hand slaps the back beneath the right armpit towards the scapula (9-1). Switch arms and sides after each slap; slap 10 times. When slapping the shoulders, keep the hands and the elbows relaxed.

Functions:

This exercise stimulates the points on the Large Intestine Meridian on the shoulders and the Small Intestine Meridian under the armpit. It can also prevent the onset of stroke and deafness.

10. Arm Rotations 手臂旋轉

10-1

(a) Step out with the left foot about 3 feet in front. Place about equal weight on both legs. Bend the left knee. Put the left hand with the thumb pointing outward and the 4 fingers resting on the inside of the leg, *Laogong* on the *Futu* point (ST 32) on the stomach meridian. Keep the back straight. Lift the right arm to shoulder height with the thumb pointing to the sky (10-1). Use the strength from the shoulder and rotate the arm upward, backward, downward, and forward. Rotate in a circular path for a total of 10 full rotations. Relax the arm and elbow – do not use any strength when rotating.

Dayan Qigong
Basic Warm Ups and Massage

10-2

(b) Keeping the feet in the same position, rotate the right arm in the opposite direction. The little finger points down and the arm rotates downward, to the back and upwards 10 times.

(c) Reverse feet by turning on the heels 180° and rotate the left arm 10 times in both the up and down directions (10-2).

Functions:
This exercise moves the muscles on the arms and the shoulders. It also moves the chest and the region of the ribs to help prevent breast cancer. When the arms and elbows are relaxed while doing the rotation, the Qi and blood flow toward the tips of the fingers. By doing so, poor circulation and nerve atrophy in the fingers can be prevented. It also prevents and treats high blood pressure and heart diseases.

11. Slap Kidneys and *Jianjing* 腎臟和肩井穴拍打

11-1

11-2

Keep the body position as in Arm Rotations. Lift the right arm to about the height of the shoulder with the right palm facing down. Bring the left arm behind the back, the palms facing out. Now slap the left *Jianjing* point (on the Gallbladder Meridian GB 21) with the outside of the right thumb (11-1) and slap the right kidney with the back of the left hand (11-2).

Switch hands and slap the opposite points. Slap 10 times. Now reverse feet by turning body 180° and slap 10 more times.

Functions:

This exercise vibrates the kidneys to stimulation the function of the kidney. Slapping the *Jianjing* (on the Gallbladder Meridian) helps to reduce fatigue and restore energy.

Dayan Qigong
Basic Warm Ups and Massage

12. Standing Massage of the Upper Body 上身按摩

12-a

a. Massage the Kidneys and *Mingmen* 腎臟和命門按摩

Stand straight with feet together. Relax the whole body. Place each hand on each kidney (12-a). Massage the entire kidney in a circular motion for 10 seconds or until the kidneys feel warm. Then place the fingers of each hand on the *Mingmen* and rub the *Mingmen* point with the finger tips for 10 seconds. The *Mingmen* is located below the 2nd lumbar vertebrae directly behind the naval. It is located on the Du Meridian and crosses 12 meridians; therefore it is sometimes referred to as the "back" *Dantian*.

This benefits the kidney functions, the *Mingmen* (DU4 or GV4) point, and the adrenal glands. Also strengthens the muscles along the lumbar vertebrae.

12-b

b. Massage the *Dabao* 大包穴按摩

The *Dabao* (SP21) point is located on the lateral side of the chest between the 6th and 7th rib.

Rub the *Dabao* points in a circular motion with the palms for 10 times (12-b)

This helps digestion function of the spleen and stomach.

c. Massage the Lymph Nodes 淋巴腺按摩

The lymph area is located around the groin by the lower stomach and leg.

Massage the lymph areas in a circle with the hands for 10 times (12-c).

This benefits the immune system.

12-c

Dayan Qigong
Basic Warm Ups and Massage

d. Massage the Chest 胸前按摩

12-d

Using the right hand in a circular motion, massage the left chest, clavicle and shoulder areas for 10 times. The left hand holds Qi in front of the body with palm facing up. Then switch hands and use the left hand to massage the right side for 10 times (12-d).

Massaging this area benefits the heart, and lung, and can prevent breast illnesses.

e. Massage the Scapula Area 肩後按摩

Place the right hand on the back of the left shoulder and the left hand against the right elbow (12-e1), massage the scapula area by pushing up the right elbow with the left hand for 10 seconds.

12-e1

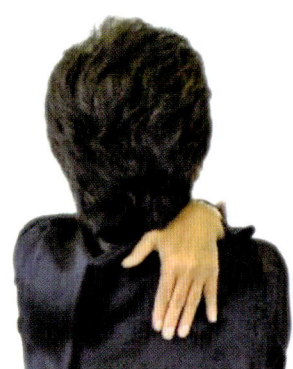

12-e2

Try to reach the *Feishu* (BL 13) point located along the scapular ridge, and *Gaohuang* (BL 43) located on the lower scapular tip (12-e2). After doing the left side, switch hands and do the right side.

Massaging this area is helpful for reducing symptoms of colds, cough, asthma, and pain in the scapula area. Massaging the *Gaohuang* point can improve general weakness caused by many illnesses.

f. Massage the Arms 手臂按摩

Extend the right arm forward with the palm facing down and fingers open. Keep the whole arm relaxed. Place the left hand on top of the right hand and rub the right hand strongly from the fingertips of the hand up to the shoulder for 10 times (12-f1 and 12-f2). Turn the right hand so the palm faces up. Rub the right arm with the left hand from the shoulder to the fingertips for 10 times (12-f3 and 12-f4). Repeat on the left arm.

This massages all of the meridians, Yin and Yang, of the hands in the direction of the Qi and blood flow.

Dayan Qigong
Basic Warm Ups and Massage

12-f1

12-f2

12-f3

12-f4

g. Rub the Back of the Hands 手背按摩

12-g

Hold the hands in front of the chest with the back sides of the hands facing up. Open the fingers and touch the right finger tips with the left finger tips. Move (rub) the left fingers down the back of the right hand, passing the *Baxie* points of the right hand which are located at the webs between the fingers (12-g). Continue to move (rub) down the back of the right hand until the *Waiguan* point. Rub a total of 10 times. Then switch hands and rub the back side of the left hand 10 times from the finger tips to the *Waiguan* point.

h. Massage the Hands 手部按摩

12-h

Open the fingers of the right hand and hold the right hand with the left hand and place the left thumb in the middle of the right hand's *Laogong* point. Using the left thumb, push up the fingers of the right hand starting from the *Laogong* to the end of each fingertip. Start on the thumb and finish on the little finger. Use enough force to bend back each finger. Keep hand up and open (12-h). Then, switch hands and massage the left hand with the right thumb.

Dayan Qigong
Basic Warm Ups and Massage

i. Shaking the Hands 抖手

12-i

After the massage, open fingers of both hands, relax the hand and shake out the wrists for 10 seconds to remove bad Qi from the hand and loosen up the fingers (12-i).

j. Massage the Back and Side of Neck 脖子按摩

12-j1

12-j2

Holding the back of the head with the left hand, use the right hand to rub the back and side of the neck (12-j1 and 12-j2).

After 10 times, switch hands, holding the head with the right hand and massaging with the left hand for 10 times.

k. Massage the Neck and Chin 脖子和下巴按摩

12-k

Place the left hand in front of the body with palm facing up. Start by placing the top side of the right index finger (on the Large Intestine Meridian) by the right side at the base of the neck and rub upwards to the chin (12-k), and then repeat the movement for a total of 10 times as the right hand moves across the neck to the left side. Then repeat from the left side of the neck to the right side for 10 times. Always start from the base of the neck. Switch hands and repeat the rubbing using the left hand.

Dayan Qigong
Basic Warm Ups and Massage

1. Massaging Points in the Head 頭部重要穴位按摩

12-l1

1. ***Taiyang*** point is located in the depression about one inch posterior to the midpoint between the lateral end of the eyebrow and the outer canthus. Rub the *Taiyang* points in a circular motion with the finger tips for about 10 seconds (12-l1).

Massaging this point is good for alleviating headaches and eye diseases.

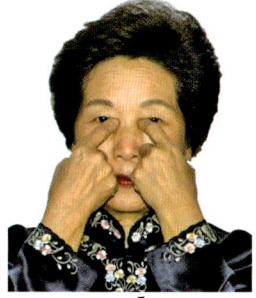

12-l2

2. ***Jingming*** (BL 1) is located on the Bladder Meridian near the inner canthus in the depression towards the nose (12-l2)

Massaging this point is good for alleviating redness and swelling of the eye, night blindness, and blurred vision.

12-l3

3. ***Yingxiang*** (LI 20) is located on the Large Intestine Meridian in the nasolabial groove where the end of the nose flares up against the maxilla (12-l3)

Massaging this point opens the nasal passage relieving nasal obstruction, running nose, bloody nose, itching and swelling of the face, and sinus related problems.

12-l4

4. Massage around the lips with the two fingers will massage many meridians that go around the mouth and improve Qi and blood circulation. Massage back and forth using the right hand starting from the right side of the mouth to the left (12-l4). Then repeat using the left hand for the mouth.

Hold the Qi at waist level with the opposite hand.

12-l5

5. Massage the outside of the ear, pinching and massaging the pinna from top to bottom. The ear represents energy flow of the whole body and massaging the ear is similar to massaging the whole body (12-l5).

12-l6

6. The ear is a representation of a fetus in the womb. Massaging the ear is like massaging the body and all the parts.

Use the two index fingers to massage all areas inside the ears (12-l6).

12-l7

7. Using the middle finger in front of the ear and index finger behind the ear, massage upward around the ear for 10 times. Do not massage downward (12-l7).
This stimulates the Small Intestine, Gallbladder, Stomach, and Triple Warm Meridians.

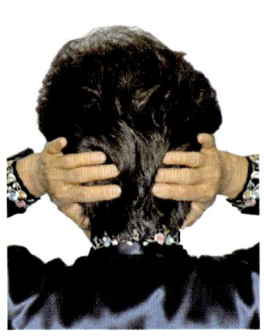

12-l8

8. Beating the Drums of Heaven. Place both palms tightly over the ears and pat the back of the head with the fingers (12-l8). This is called the Drums of Heaven. This stimulates the many meridians that go to the back of the head. Drumming this area is good for hearing and the Du Meridian.

Dayan Qigong
Basic Warm Ups and Massage

12-l9

9. Wash face and comb hair

Relax both hands and place both hands below the chin and move hands up the face. Hands can either touch the face or about 1 inch away from the face. Continue moving hands from the face up to the *Baihui* point, then turn the hands so fingers point toward each other and slowly move the hand down the back of the head and neck. Then move hands to the front and turn the palms to one another, and then separate the hands to move the hands up the face again, giving Qi to the face, etc. Do this for 10 times (12-l9).

Wash face and comb hair is giving the Qi to the face and head.

Shake out hands before starting at the chin position if feeling any sickness.

13. One Leg Stand 金雞獨立

13-1

13-2

Stand on the right leg with the leg slightly bent and the right foot flat on the ground. Slowly raise the left knee up to the chest. Wrap the left arm around the tibia and hold the foot with the right hand (13-1). . Hold for 10 seconds, and slowly place foot on the ground Repeat on the other side. Do not lose balance.

After practicing for a while, then repeat a second time, only this time bend the leg the weight is on and try to slowly come down to the ground with the foot that is being held (13-2). Slowly come back up, and repeat on the other side.

Beginners should only practice the first part; only do the second part when the balance and strength have improved.

Functions:

This exercise is for strengthening the legs' elasticity and flexibility, and also for balancing the whole body.

14. Squats and Stretches 橫拔筋

14-1

Separate the legs about 3-4 feet apart (or as far as comfortable). Extend the right leg to the side, keeping it straight. Bend the left leg and squat down. Keep the feet on the ground throughout the exercise. Grab the opposite elbow with each hand and push down toward the ground 10 times. Keep the back straight (14-1).

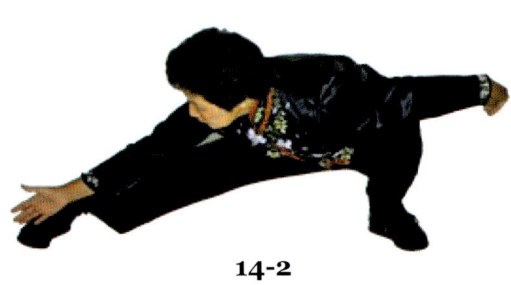
14-2

Then open the arms, keeping the legs positioned the same as above, stretch your right arm towards the right foot (14-2). Open and relax the fingers of the right hand. On the left hand, fingers point to the ground. The body follows the direction of the stretching, whether leaning forward or squatting downward. Stretch 10 times toward the right foot. Come back to the center and then repeat on the left side.

Functions:

This is an exercise for lateral stretching the legs, waist, back, and arms. It is mainly for increasing the strength in the lumbar region and the legs.

15. Walking Kicks (Heel and Toe) 動步踢腿

(a) Heel Kicks:

15-1

Stand with the feet together. Place the hands on kidneys. Take a step forward and to the left with the left foot. Flex the right foot upward and kick diagonally toward the left side of the body in a 45° position. When kicking, bend the knee and use the strength from the knee to kick out with the heel. Bring the leg back and place the foot on the ground to the right side, and then kick the left heel diagonally towards the right. Kick alternately to each side for 10 times, 10 steps (15-1).

Dayan Qigong
Basic Warm Ups and Massage

(b) Toe Kicks:

Stand and place the hands as in the Heel Kicks. Take a step forward and to the left with the left foot. Point the right toe downward and kick diagonally toward the left side of the body in a 45° position. When kicking, bend the knee and use the strength from the knee to kick out with the toe. Bring the leg back and place the foot on the ground to the right, and then kick the left toe diagonally towards the right. Kick alternately to each side for 10 times for 10 steps (15-2).

Function:

15-2

Strengthens the legs, knees, heels, and toes, and improves walking balance.

16. Walking Kick Heel 踢腳跟

16-1

16-2

Take a step with the right foot and kick the Achilles tendon with the toes of the left foot. Step with the left foot and kick the Achilles tendon with the toes of the right foot. Continue this walking and heel kicking for 10 times on each side (16-1 and 16-2).

This benefits the toes and tendon to make the legs stronger.

17. Walking

Walk normally while gathering the Qi to the lower *Dantian*. Concentrate on the palms and lower *Dantian*. Walk slower, step heel down first, then *Yongquan* and toes, and let each *Laogong* hold the Qi to the lower *Dantian*, like walking meditation. Walk 20 steps (17-1 and 17-2).

This improves walking balance and concentration, and increase the energy of the lower *Dantian*.

17-1

17-2

18. Sitting Massages 坐姿穴位按摩 (If more information is needed on finding the points or meridians, refer to the Meridian and Points Section of the book)

a. *Yongquan* 湧泉 (KI 1) is located on the Kidney Meridian on the bottom of the foot in the depression below the second and third toes, behind the ball of the foot.

Use the thumb to massage for 10 seconds (18-a).

Massaging this point is helpful in increasing kidney energy, reduces headaches, blurring of vision, sore throat, dryness of the tongue, loss of voice, and feet problems.

18-a

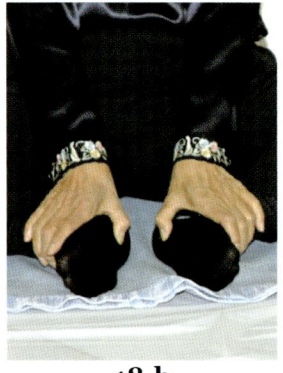

b. *Shimian* 失眠 is a special point. This point is located 2 inches from heel in the center.

Use the thumb to massage for 10 seconds (18-b).

Massaging this point is helpful for insomnia, heel pain, and heel spurs.

18-b

c. Massaging the entire arch of the foot is massaging many of the meridians that are going to the foot.

Use the thumb to massage for 10 seconds (18-c).

This massage is good for prevention of some cancers.

18-c

18-d

d. Sanyinjiao 三陰交 (SP 6) is located on the Spleen Meridian, 3 inches directly above the medial malleolus, and posterior to the medial border of the tibia. This point is where 3 Yin meridians cross (spleen, liver, and kidney).

Use the thumb to massage for 10 seconds (18-d).

Massaging this point is helpful for abdominal pain, gas, abdominal dissension, diarrhea, dysmenorrhea, irregular menstruation, many hormonal problems, enuresis, dysuria, edema, headache, dizziness, vertigo, and insomnia.

18-e

e. Zusanli 足三里 (ST 36) is located on the Stomach Meridian, 3 inches from the hollow (dimple) on the lateral side of the patella to the depression where the tibia and fibula meets.

Use the thumb to massage for 10 seconds (18-e).

Massaging this point is helpful with gastric pain, vomiting, hiccups, abdominal distension, gas, diarrhea, dysentery, constipation, aching of the knee joint and leg, edema, cough, asthma, indigestion, dizziness, insomnia.

18-f

f. Liangqiu 梁丘 (ST 34) is located on the Stomach Meridian, 2 inches above the patella, just slightly lateral to the femur bone.

Use the thumb to massage for 10 seconds (18-f).

Massaging this point is helpful for pain, numbness, and stiffness of the knee, cold feet, gastric pain, mastitis, and back problems.

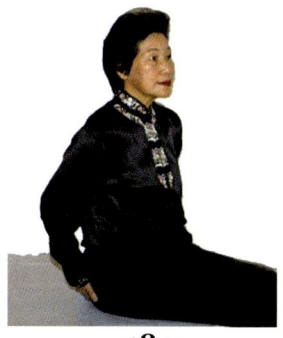

18-g

g. Huantiao 環跳 (GB 30) is located on the Gallbladder Meridian in the dimple of the buttocks, near the big joint of the hip. The point is very deep.

Use the hand to massage for 10 seconds (18-g).

Massaging this point is helpful for relieving pain in the lumbar region, and thigh, and treats sciatica problems.

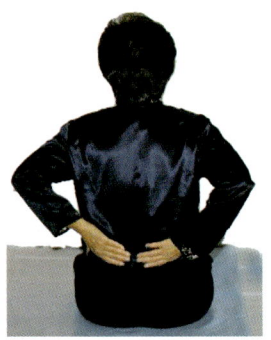

h. Massage the Kidneys 腎臟按摩
Massaging the kidneys with hands in a circular motion for 10 seconds is helpful for relieving stiffness of the back, lumbar pain, diarrhea, indigestion, weakness of the knees, dizziness, blurring of vision, tinnitus, deafness, edema, and asthma (18-h)

18-h

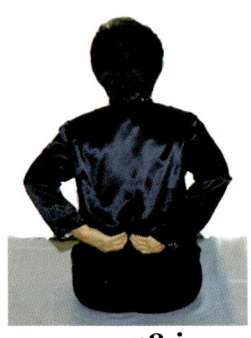

i. *Mingmen* 命門 (DU 4) is located on the Du Meridian. The *Mingmen* point is located below the spinous process of the second lumbar vertebrae, behind the navel (18-i).

Use the finger tips to massage for 10 seconds.

Massaging this point is helpful for stiffness of the back, lumbar pain, diarrhea, and indigestion.

18-i

Reminder: All of the following points are symmetrical or one on each side. Therefore, remember to do both sides. Also, references to "inches" in the text refer to one's body inches.

j. *Laogong* 勞宮 (PC 8) is located on the Pericardium Meridian at the center of the palm, between the middle and ring finger, when a fist is made.

Use the thumb to massage for 10 seconds (18-j).

Massaging this point is helpful in alleviating cardiac pain, gastritis, foul breath, vomiting, and nausea.

18-i8-j

k. *Hegu* 合谷 (LI 4) is located on the Large Intestine Meridian on the dorsum of the hand between the 1st and 2nd metacarpal bones, on the radial side, in the middle of the 2nd metacarpal. Use the thumb to pinch the *Hegu* point for 10 seconds (18-k). Massaging this point is helpful for headaches, pain in the neck, redness, swelling and pain in the eye, nasal obstruction, running nose, toothache, deafness, swelling of the face, sore throat, abdominal pain, and constipation. **Note**: Pregnant women should **not** massage this point.

18-k

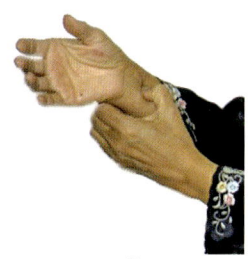

l. Neiguan 內關 (PC 6) is located on the Pericardium Meridian located 2 inches above the transverse crease of the wrist between the two tendons.

Massage for 10 seconds (18-l).

18-l

Massaging this point is helpful for cardiac pain, palpitation, stomachache, nausea, vomiting, hiccup, insomnia. Also helps to improve memory loss due to stroke, chest pains, anxiety, flushing in the face, abdominal pain and heartburn.

m. Chize 尺澤 (LU 5) is located on the Lung Meridian, halfway between the middle of the elbow and the lateral side of the elbow in the crease (18-m).

Use the thumb to massage for 10 seconds.

Massaging this point is helpful for cough, asthma, sore throat, mastitis, and tendonitis

18-m

n. Quepen 缺盆 (ST 12) and **Qihu** 氣戶 (ST 13) are located on the Stomach Meridian with the *Quepen* in the midpoint of the supra-clavicular fossa, and the *Qihu* below the clavicle in the middle (18-n)

Use the fingers on top of clavicle for *Quepen* and thumbs on bottom for *Qihu* to massage for 10 seconds.

18-n

Massaging this point is helpful for relieving cough, asthma, sore throat, hiccup, and pain in the chest and back.

o. Dabao 大包 (SP 21) is located on Spleen Meridian on the lateral side of the chest between the 6th and 7th rib.

Use the palms to rub circles around the *Dabao* point for 10 seconds (18-o).

Massaging this point is helpful for pain in the chest, asthma, general aching and weakness.

18-o

p. Massage the Lower *Dantian*

Overlap the two hands on top of the naval. With the right hand on the inside, massage by moving around the naval for 10 seconds in clockwise direction. Then, with the left hand inside, massage in the counterclockwise direction for 10 seconds (18-p).

This massages all the organs and meridians around the lower *Dantian*.

18-p

19. Legs and Body Stretching (to be done after sitting meditation)
腿和身體拔筋

a. Elbows to Ankles

Stretch forward 10 times, holding the elbows and touch the ankles. Toes are pointing up towards chest. Keep the legs straight (19-a).

This is good to strengthen the legs and back for better flexibility.

19-a

b. Wrap Hands Around Heels

Hold heels with both hands and put head down on the legs, for 10 seconds (19-b).

19-b

This exercise strengthens and lengthens the legs and back, for better flexibility.

c. Knee to Chest

Bring knee up to chest with heel toward the hip area and toes pointing down. Hold for 10 seconds. Do this for both sides 19-c).
This is for better balance and strengthens the thigh, leg and back.

19-c

d. Ankle Rotations

Straighten out the legs and rotate ankles outward for 10 times, then repeat rotating the ankles inward for 10 times (19-d).

19-d

This strengthens the ankles and all the meridians that go around the ankles, and helps in preventing ankle injuries such as sprains and weakness in these joints.

Master Shao, Master Chiang, Master Liu, and Grandmaster Yang in 2002

Master Liu with students doing sit down massage

Dayan Qigong
Summary of Dayan Qigong 64 Movements
大雁氣功 前 64 式

1. Starting Form 起式
2. Stretch Wings 展翅
3. Close Wings 合翅
4. Push and Set the Wings 折窩
5. Shake Upper Arms 抖膀
6. Push and Set the wings 折窩
7. Shake Upper arms 抖膀
8. Lift 上舉
9. Close Hands 合掌
10. Turn Hands 翻掌
11. Bend 下腰
12. Turn Hands 纏手
13. Restore Qi 回氣
14. Push Forefoot 左彈足
15. Push Qi 推氣
16. Scoop Up the Qi 撈氣
17. Turn Around and Restore Qi 轉身回氣
18. Push Forefoot 右彈足
19. Push Qi 推氣
20. Scoop Up the Qi 撈氣
21. Turn Hands 纏手
22. Waving Hands Like Clouds 雲手
23. Rinse Waist 涮腰
24. Fall Upon Arm and Restore Qi 落膀回氣
25. Stretch Single Wing 單展翅
26. Step Up and Raise Arm 上步伸膀
27. Wrap Head to Ear 纏頭過耳
28. Push Down 下壓
29. Hold Up 上托
30. Restore Qi 回氣
31. Drag Moon From Water 撈月
32. Turn Around 轉身
33. Step Up and Look at the Palm 上步望掌
34. Look At the Moon 望月
35. Push Qi 壓氣
36. Turn and Push Qi 轉身壓氣
37. Swim 泳動
38. Bird's-eye View of the Water 瞰水
39. Fly Over Water 拍水飛翔
40. Drink Water 飲水
41. Look at the Sky 望天
42. Restore Qi 歸氣
43. Grasp Qi 抓氣
44. Grasp Qi (palm up) 翻掌撈氣
45. Hold the Ball 抱球
46. Massage the Ball 揉球
47. Turn and Massage the Ball 轉身揉球
48. Hold the Qi 抱氣
49. Penetrate Qi 貫氣
50. Raise Arms 抬膀
51. Turn Wings 翻翅
52. Put the Wings on Back 背翅
53. Fly Up 起扇上飛
54. Turn around 轉身
55. Fly Up 飛上
56. Fly Over Water 過水飛翔
57. Turn Around 轉身
58. Fly Up 飛上
59. Search Food 尋食
60. Turn Around 轉身
61. Seeking Nest 尋窩
62. Turn Around and Swim 轉身泳動
63. Restore Qi and Sleep 安睡歸氣
64. Close Form 收式

Dayan Qigong
64 Movements: Specific Instructions

Form 1: Starting Form 起式

1-1

Begin with both feet together, arms at your sides. Shift your weight to one foot and place the nonweighted foot under its corresponding shoulder. Now shift your weight so that you are balanced equally on both feet. Stand erect with feet parallel and shoulder width apart (1-1). Let the arms and hands hang naturally at the sides with elbows slightly bent. Keep the wrists straight with the palms about 1 inch from the legs, fingers open and slightly curled and thumbs open. (*Hegu* is open). Relax the face, with the tongue touching the upper palette behind the teeth to connect the Ren meridian with the Du meridian. (Back teeth are slightly touching each other, but not clenched.) Relax the shoulders, the arms, the legs, and concentrate on the lower *Dantian* for a short moment. Clear the mind, looking forward and seeing nothing (by not paying attention to the surrounding views and sound) and concentrating on the movements.

Form 2: Stretch Wings 展翅

2-1   2-2   2-3   2-4

Bend the body forward. The hands naturally go backward so the palms face the *Huantiao* points (GB 30), and then the arms and fingers travel downwards by the sides of the legs, past the knees, and preferably below the knees to the ankles (2-1).) The hands do not touch the legs as they come down for this movement.

After passing the knees (2-2), stand up with the arms outstretched, palms facing each other, shoulder width apart, and looking at both hands.

Bring both hands up to shoulder height. (2-3)

Continue the upwards movement while separating and opening the hands. At the same time raise the heels, extend the arms with the palms facing the sky, and elbows slightly curled. Bend

Dayan Qigong
64 Movements: Specific Instructions

the body backwards and look at the sky. Be careful to maintain balance and not to bend too far back. The feeling should be as if holding a giant Qi ball on the arms, chest, and chin. (2-4)

Form 3:   Close Wings 合翅

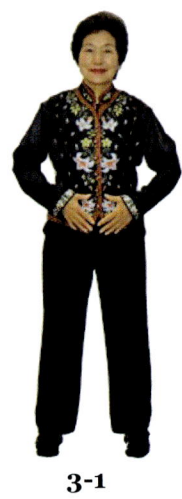

3-1

3-2

Return to upright stance and bring the hands down towards the lower *Dantian* in a sweeping motion. At the same time heels come down slowly and both hands are close to the lower *Dantian*. (3-1)

Drop the fingers down naturally (3-2)

Form 4:   Push and Set the Wings 折窩

Keeping the hands relaxed, move the hands to the middle of the chest. (4-1)

Turn hands with fingertips pointing upward, still palm to palm. (4-2) Look at both hands and push out slowly, focusing on the fingers, wrists, elbows and then the shoulders.

The body will follow as you push out (4-3)

Rotate the hands, thumbs pointing down (4-4). Push back slowly, rotating the shoulders and bring the arms back slowly in a sweeping motion. Raise both heels. When the arms get to the back, close the fingers to form claws (the thumb is touching the first joint of the middle finger and the rest of the fingers close around the thumb and middle finger – this is known as the bird's claw).

Dayan Qigong
64 Movements: Specific Instructions

4-1

4-2

4-3

4-4

Form 5: Shake Upper Arms 抖膀

5-1

5-2

5-3

Bring the hands (claws) to the kidneys with the *Hegu* points touching the kidneys, located on either side of the spine, above the waist (5-1)

Relax and open the position of the fingers. (5-2)

Slide the hands, with the *Hegu* still touching the waist, to the side of the waist.

Now flip the hands out forward with the palms facing upward, and drop the heels quickly to the floor at the same time. The elbows should be touching the waist and at a 90° angle (5-3). The fingers should be open, and the eyes are looking forward.

This form rids the stagnant Qi in the kidney and gallbladder meridians.

Dayan Qigong
64 Movements: Specific Instructions

Form 6: Push and Set the Wings 折窩

6-1

6-2

6-3

6-4

Lift both hands to about chest height at the level of the *Qihu* points, with the fingers pointing up (6-1).

Look at both hands and push out slowly, focusing on the fingers, wrists, elbows, and then the shoulders. (6-2) The body will follow as the hands push out.

Turn the hands out (6-3), then push back slowly, by rotating the shoulders and bring the arms back slowly in a sweeping motion. Raise both heels. When the arms get to the back, close the fingers to form claws (the thumb is touching the first joint of the middle finger and the rest of the fingers close around the thumb and middle finger

Bring the hands (claws) to the kidneys with the *Hegu* points touching the kidneys, located on either side of the spine, above the waist

Relax and open the position of the fingers.

Slide the hands, with the *Hegu* still touching the waist, to the side of the waist.

Now flip the hands out forward with the palms facing upward, and drop the heels quickly to the floor at the same time. The elbows should be touching the waist and at a 90° angle (6-4). The fingers should be open, and the eyes are looking forward.

This is a repeat of Form 4.

Form 7: Shake Upper Arms 抖膀

7-1

Repeat Form 5 and end with the arms at 90 ° beside the body. (7-1)

Form 8: Lift 上舉

8-1

8-2

Lift the arms up so the fingers are at the chin level (8-1).

Bring the hands straight up past the face, to the *Baihui* point at about 1 inch above the top of the head, with the elbows facing forward.

This gives Qi to the face and the *Baihui* point (8-2).

Form 9: Close Hands 合掌

9-1

Now open the elbows to the sides and interlace the fingers. Touch the thumbs together.

Hold the hands over the *Baihui* point (9-1).

Form 10: Turn Hands Over 翻掌

10-1

With fingers still interlaced and thumbs touching each other, turn the palms to face the sky.

Push the hands straight up above the *Baihui* point and straighten the arms.

With the hands pushed up, the eyes look up into the sky, but do not tilt the head back. Make sure the hands remain directly above the *Baihui* point (10-1).

Form 11: Bend 下腰

11-1   **11-2**   **11-3**

Bend the body forward at the hips, with back, legs, and arms straight; push straight down with the hands to the floor in front of the feet. Look at both hands (11-1).

Then lift your hands, to knee height with the fingers still interlaced. Do not raise the body.

Then, turn the upper body to the left, keeping the feet still. Press palms down outside the toes of the left foot (11-2).

Then, lift the hands straight up to knee height, turn the upper body to the right side (do not raise the body), and press the palms down outside the toes of the right foot (11-3).

Move the body back to the center by rotating the hips and moving the hands back to the center between the feet. Look at the hands. The position of the feet remains unchanged throughout (11-1)

Note: Try to touch the floor with the interlaced hands, but do not over-exert the body. Rather than forcing the body down, try to relax first. If it is difficult to reach all the way to the floor, then think of the hands touching the floor. In any case, keep the legs straight. Flexibility should improve with practice.

Dayan Qigong
64 Movements: Specific Instructions

Form 12: Turn Hands 纏手

12-1   12-2

Open the hands and push out to the side of each foot, about one foot away from the lateral side of each foot (12-1).

Looking at both hands, turn palm to palm. (12-2)

Form 13: Restore Qi 回氣

13-1   13-2   13-3   13-4

Turn the body about 45° to the left while turning on the left foot's *Yongquan* point, with the left heel off the floor. At the same time, bend both elbows and move the right hand under the left elbow. Look at the left palm (13-1).

Dayan Qigong
64 Movements: Specific Instructions

Starting with the *Laogong* point of the right hand under the left elbow, move both arms so that the right palm slides under the left forearm with the left arm moving towards the body as the right hand moves out underneath the left forearm. The arms do not tough one another during the entire movement.

As the right arm is moving out, shift the body weight forward to the left foot, keeping the leg straight and place the left foot flat on the floor. At the same time, the right heel comes off the floor.

Continue the forward thrust until the left hand is near the right elbow.

Move the left hand's *Laogong* point under your right elbow, and pass the left palm under the right forearm (13-2). At the same time shift body weight back to the right foot, bend the left knee, and place the heel of the right foot flat on the floor; lift the toes while the left heel touches the floor. Now the left leg is straight and the right leg is bent.

Bring the left hand upwards toward the body while making a claw with the left hand, and point the claw to the *Quepen* point just above the middle of the left clavicle (13-3).

Look at the right hand, drop the hand down, and sweep the right arm backwards in a circular motion while straightening up the body to a standing position (13-4), then again bend the body forward as the right hand completes the big circle to grab the left toes (14-1).

When sweeping the right arm (13-4), always point the right palm towards the direction of the left toes. Keep the circular motion of the right arm in one plane in-line with the body.

Form 14: Push Left Forefoot 左彈足 (3 times)

14-1

The right thumb is pressing on to the first and second left toes and the other 4 fingers are tightly holding the bottom of the left foot.

With the left fingers in the claw and positioned on the *Quepen* and the right hand holding the left foot, massage the foot and *Quepen* by making 3 turns with both elbows – the left elbow turns up and out, and the right elbow turns down and out (14-1). The shoulders also turn in harmony following the turns of the elbows.

Note: For the more experienced students, make 3 circles with both elbows – the left elbow turns counter-clockwise and the right elbow turns counter-clockwise.

Apply as much strength as is comfortable.

Dayan Qigong
64 Movements: Specific Instructions

If grasping the toes is difficult, then simply point the fingers of the right hand toward the left toes, then turn the waist and thrust the elbows, while imagining the right hand grasping the toes.

Form 15: Push Qi 推氣

15-1

The right hand releases the left foot. Place the left foot flat on the floor, then raise the left heel and turn on the left *Yongquan* point until the left foot becomes parallel with the right foot.

At the same time, the right hand pushes the Qi out 1 foot to the right side, and 6 inches in front of the right toes (15-1).

Form 16: Scoop up the Qi 撈氣

16-1

Turn the right hand so the palm faces inward, then scoop up the Qi to the front of the body, palm up.

Look at the right hand.

The body remains in the bent position (16-1).

Dayan Qigong
64 Movements: Specific Instructions

Form 17: Turn Around and Restore Qi 轉身回氣

17-1   17-2

Bring the right hand up, and close the fingers to form a claw, and then point on the right *Quepen* point above the middle of the clavicle bone (17-1).

Drop the left hand from the *Quepen*. As the left hand comes down, bring the right toes up. Look at the left hand and start to make the big circle as the body straightens up – let the hand lead the body to stand up
(17-2).

While making the circular motion with the left arm, always point the left palm towards the right toes. This is the same as Form 13 only on the reverse side of the body.

Form 18: Push Right Forefoot 右彈足 (3 times)

Bring left hand down quickly to the right toes. The thumb is on the first and the second toes, and the other four fingers are on the bottom of the toes (18-1).

With the right fingers in a claw positioned on the *Quepen* and the left hand holding the right toes, massage the toes and *Quepen* by making 3 turns with both elbows – the left elbow turns up and out, and the right elbow turns down and out. The shoulders also turn in harmony following the turns of the elbows.

18-1

Dayan Qigong
64 Movements: Specific Instructions

This is the same as Form 14 reversed.

Note: For the more experienced students, make 3 circles with both elbows – the left elbow turns clockwise and the right elbow turns clockwise.

The stomach, liver, and spleen meridians pass through the first and second toes. The *Quepen* is also on the stomach meridian. Therefore, this form is very beneficial for circulation to the stomach, liver, and spleen meridians.

Form 19: Push Qi 推氣

The left hand releases the right foot. Turn on the right heel to bring the right foot in parallel with the left foot.

At the same time, the left hand pushes the Qi out to the left side 1 foot to the left and 6 inches in front of the left toes (19-1).

19-1

Form 20: Scoop Up the Qi 撈氣

20-1

20-2

Turn left palm and bring arm back to the center.

Dayan Qigong
64 Movements: Specific Instructions

Stand up, holding the Qi. (20-1)

Look at left hand.

The right palm opens so the side of the little finger is near the Ren meridian.

With the right little finger on the Ren meridian, bring the right hand down the middle of the body, lower than the left hand. (20-2)

Form 21: Turn Hands 纏手

21-1

21-2

21-3

Continue to bring the right hand down the middle of the body. As the right hand passes the left hand, raise the left hand up so the left palm faces the middle *Dantian* while the right hand moves down to the lower *Dantian* (21-1). Both palms face the body (21-2)

The right hand is slightly above the waist at the right side. The right hand moves up while the left hand moves down. Continue the circular motion by moving the right hand down while the left hand moves up. Finally, the left hand moves down to the middle *Dantian* and then moves to the left side of the waist. Look at the right palm at the end of the movement (21-3).

The hand that moves down is on the inside closer to the body while the hand that moves up is on the outside.

Form 22: Wave Hands Like Clouds (Right, Left, Right) 雲手 (右, 左, 右)

22-1   22-2   22-3   22-4

The right hand comes out to the front of the body at waist height, and the right foot comes out at the same time and lands one foot in front. The outside of the right foot is touching the floor at the side of *Yongquan* point. The body weight is on the back leg (left leg) (22-1).

Sweep the right hand to the right and to the back at waist height while the waist turns also turns following the arm movement (22-2). When the right hand moves to a diagonal line behind the body, rotate the right hand so the *Hegu* point points to the body, then bend the elbow to bring the right hand to the right kidney. Rest the *Hegu* point on the right kidney.

Throughout this movement, the eyes should follow the right hand as it extends outward. Right before the hand goes to the kidney, turn the head and body to face forward.

Shift the body weight to the right foot. Bring the right heel in which will "massage" the right *Yongquan* point, place right heel down, and step out with the left foot one foot in front (22-3). The outside of the left foot touches the floor at the side of *Yongquan* point. The body's weight is on the back leg (right leg). At the same time, move the left hand/arm forward and sweep to the left side of the body. The waist turns to follow the left hand. When the left hand moves to a diagonal line behind the body, rotate the left hand so that the *Hegu* point points to the body, then bend the elbow to bring the left hand to the left kidney, with the *Hegu* point resting on the left kidney.

Now both *Hegu* points should be on the kidneys. (22-4).

Dayan Qigong
64 Movements: Specific Instructions

22-5   **22-6**

Right before the hand goes to the kidneys, turn the head and body to face forward. Repeat the right side again by taking a step forward with the right foot (left heel turning in, "massaging" the left *Yongquan*) and extending the right arm. Move the hand to the right side and then to the back; the eyes follow the right hand. Turn at the waist (22-5).

When the right hand moves to a diagonal line behind the body, rotate the right hand so the *Hegu* point points to the right kidney, then bend the elbow to bring the right *Hegu* point to the kidney. Again, both *Hegu* points are on the kidneys (22-6), with the right leg still forward.

Note: Placing the foot on the floor with only the outside edge of the ball of the foot touching the floor opens a very important point on the bottom of the foot in the center—the *Yongquan* point (KI 1), the first point of the kidney meridian. This foot position is used often in the set. It is often referred as open the *Yongquan* point.

Form 23: Rinse Waist 涮腰

23-1

23-2

23-3

23-4

23-5

Step forward with the left foot. The left hand comes out (23-1) and goes to the side. Look at the left hand.

When the left hand gets to the side, move the right hand out to the side with the fingers pointing downward (23-2).

Dayan Qigong
64 Movements: Specific Instructions

Turn the body to the left (23-3), and bring the right hand to the face with the right *Hegu* point facing the upper *Dantian*. The left *Hegu* faces the lower back with the fingers pointing to the right heel (23-4). The body turns to the left with the movement of the arms.

During the turning of the body, stand up on both *Yongquan* points with both heels up. (Or, just lift the right heel if balance is difficult). Most of the weight is on the left leg.

At the end of the turn, look both at the left hand and at the right heel. (23-4)

Turn the left hand so the palm is facing forward, then quickly bring the palm to face the upper *Dantian* at 1 foot away from the upper *Dantian*. This holds the Qi and gives Qi to the upper *Dantian*.

At the same time, bring the right arm and hand to the waist at 90°. All the weight is on the back leg. The outside of the left foot touches the floor at the *Yongquan* point (23-5).

Form 24: Drop Arm to Recover Qi 落膀回氣

Look at the left hand (24-1) and turn the left hand (palm) down (24-2).

24-1

24-2

24-3

Raise your chest slightly as the thumb follows the Ren meridian down to the lower *Dantian*. Look straight ahead. (24-2)

Continue to move the left hand from the lower *Dantian* to the left side until the left *Hegu* faces the left *Huantiao* (24-3). Keep left hand about 1 inch from the *Huantiao*.

Form 25: Stretch Single Wing 單展翅

25-1   25-2   25-3

Shift the weight to the left leg, extend the right hand and arm to shoulder high, and step forward with the right foot with the *Yongquan* point open (25-1).

Sweep the right hand to the right side at shoulder height, eyes follow the right hand (25-2).

Continue to move the right hand to the back and place the right *Hegu* on the right kidney, look straight ahead (25-3).

Form 26: Step up and Raise Arm 上步伸膀

26-1

Shift the weight to the right leg, and step forward with the left foot with the *Yongquan* point open.

Bring the left hand to the waist by making a little circle with the left hand and keeping the fingers straight. Rest the hand at 90° to the body

Eyes are looking at the left hand (26-1).

Form 27: Wrap Head to Ear 纏頭過耳

27-1

27-2

27-3

Wrap the right hand around the waist using the right *Hegu* point – starting from the kidney, follow along the waist to the front of the body, cross over the Ren meridian, over and up the left hand with the right *Laogong* facing the left *Hegu*. Now move the right *Laogong* up to the left shoulder (27-1), and up to the left ear (27-2).

Give Qi to the left ear, then around the back of the head. Then give qi to the right ear (27-3).

Form 28: Push Down 下壓

28-1

28-2

From the right ear, the right hand pushes down to the back. As the right hand lowers, the elbow stays slightly bent and the right *Hegu* faces the right *Huantiao* (28-1). As the right hand is at waist height, the left hand will start to come up.

The left hand comes up to *Qihu*'s height (28-2), one and a half foot away from *Qihu* point. Look at left hand.

Shift the weight to the left leg.

Form 29: Hold Up 上托

29-1 **29-2**

Turn the right hand so the palm is facing forward and at the same time the weight changes to the left leg with the right heel raised (29-1).

While shifting the weight to the left leg, lower the left hand to the hip while turning the left hand so the *Hegu* is facing the *Huantiao*. At the same time, raise the right hand so the *Laogong* is facing the right *Qihu*. Look at the right hand (29-2).

Form 30: Restore Qi 回氣

Turn the left shoulder so the arm and palm face forward. Then quickly bring up the left hand to the upper *Dantian*; *Laogong* faces the upper *Dantian,* one foot far.

At the same time, close the right fingers into a claw and place it on the right *Quepen* point. Look at the left hand (30-1).

30-1

Form 31: Drag Moon from the Water 撈月

31-1   31-2   31-3

Turn the head to the right rear corner and open the fingers of the right hand (31-1). While opening the right hand, let the fingers bring the arm out, with the hand higher than the head, and with a slight curve in the elbow. Look at the right hand as it goes out.

At the same time, move the left hand closer to the left ear, about one inch from the ear (32-2).

In a scooping movement, drop the right hand in a circle to the front, eyes following the right hand (31-3).

31-4   31-5

The right hand's *Laogong* faces the left leg's *Sanyinjiao*, and the left hand faces the upper *Dantian* (31-4). Continue moving the right hand upward to the left until the outside of the right elbow is touching below and directly in front of the left elbow. (31-5)

Continue moving the right hand in front of the face so the *Laogong* is facing the upper *Dantian*, one foot far. The eyes follow the right hand. As the head turns to look at the right hand, the left palm faces the right ear, one inch away.

Form 32: Turn Around 轉身

Still looking at the right hand, turn on left heel 90° to the right, and then on the right heel 90° to the right. (32-1)

While turning to the right, the right hand stays at the upper *Dantian*, the left hand goes down to the middle *Dantian* (32-2), to the lower *Dantian*, then *Hegu* to *Huantiao* (32-3). At the same time, the body is rising upright.

The weight is on the left leg.

Dayan Qigong
64 Movements: Specific Instructions

Look at the right palm, keep turning to the back 180°. After the turn, the body is standing up, and the right *Laogong* is still facing the upper *Dantian* (32-4).

Right hand on upper *Dantian*, left *Hegu* on left *Huantiao*.

The left *Hegu* is facing the left *Huantiao* (32-5).

Form 33: Step Up and Look at the Palm 上步望掌

33-1

33-2

Right palm stays at the upper *Dantian*, left *Hegu* is at *Huantiao*. (33-1)

Shift the weight to the right leg.

Step forward with the left *Yongquan* open.

At the same time the left hand comes up to the waist and turn the fingers forward.

Continue to bring the left hand straight out and up to the upper *Dantian* one foot away, and right palm moves to the right *Taiyang* point 1 inch away.

Form 34: Look at the Moon 望月

34-1

34-2

34-3

The *Yongquan* side of the left foot is touching the floor.

Turn the head to the right.

Move left palm closer to the left ear. At the same time, the right hand goes out from the *Taiyang* point leading with the fingers and pointing to the right rear corner. The right hand should be higher than the head (34-1).

Look at and concentrate on the right hand while bring the arm out. Keep the right elbow slightly curled.

Scoop Qi with the right palm to the left *Sanyinjiao*, as the head turns following the movement of the right palm, the left hand now faces the upper *Dantian* (34-2)

Scoop up quickly with the right palm to the left, by placing the right arm under the left elbow and turn the head to look at the sky. The right hand faces the upper *Dantian,* one foot far and the left palm faces the right ear, one inch away (34-3).

Dayan Qigong
64 Movements: Specific Instructions

Form 35: Push Qi 壓氣 （三次）

35-1

35-2

35-3

Bring both hands to the front, bring the right leg closer to the left leg, and raise both heels. (35-1)

Turn the hands so the fingers of the two hands are facing each other, and place the hands close to the sides of the left knee (35-2).

Looking at both hands, push hands straight down to the floor following the left leg and keeping the fingers of the two hands pointed at each other (35-3).

Once down, the fingers drop down pointing to the ground and relaxed. Now raise the body slightly and bring the hands up the sides of the left leg, with the *Hegu* points facing the leg, and stop at knee height.

Push down, relax the fingers, and come up with the *Hegu*'s points facing the leg for a total of 3 times.

Note: Keep your balance. If reaching to the floor is difficult, imagine you are reaching to the floor. It may be difficult to keep the heels off the floor, but that should improve over time. In the beginning, leave the back heel down for more balance, then bring both heels up as the balance improves.

Form 36: Turn and Push Qi 轉身壓氣

36-1　　　　　　　　36-2　　　　　　　　36-3

After the 3rd time of pushing down and coming up, move *Hegu*'s points over to the side of the right knee. (36-1)

Turn both to the right 90° simultaneously using both *Yongquan* points. Heels up (36-2). (Shift the left leg back a little to be more comfortable, if necessary.)

Again, push down 3 times along the right leg, similar to Form 35 (36-3).

Form 37: Swim 泳動

37-1

37-2

After the 3rd time of pushing down, start fluttering the hands and look at both hands (37-1).

Dayan Qigong
64 Movements: Specific Instructions

Stand up with the fingers, hands, arms, and upper body all shaking together, and extend the arms upwards towards the sky. Look up to the sky and bring the arms above the head. Continue shaking the fingers, hands, arms, and upper body.

Weight is on right leg, and the back heel is up. (37-2)

The flutter in this and many following movements should be rapid but gentle. The hands shake up and down, with the fingers slightly apart. The flutter should extend to the arms and the upper body, all the way down to the waist. Keep the arms and fingers relaxed while doing this movement.

Shaking the hands is an important movement as this helps open up all the micro-meridians of the body and also "shakes" out the stagnant Qi in the body.

Form 38: Bird's-eye View of the Water 瞰水

38-1

38-2

From above the head, open the arms to the sides and sweep them down to the back, still shaking (38-1).

The body leans forward with both heels up, hands are to the back, palm facing palm with a little curl in the elbows, The eyes are looking out on the floor about 7 to 8 feet in front.
Shaking the hands to the back is giving Qi to the lower back and kidneys.

Keep the neck and back straight and relaxed (38-2).

Form 39: Fly Over Water 拍水飛翔 （左, 右, 左）

39-1  **39-2**  **39-3**  **39-4**

39-5  **39-6**  **39-7**

Now shake the hands forward to shoulder high and shoulder width apart, still shaking. Look at the left hand and move the left leg to the left rear corner (39-1).

Shake both hands to the lower *Dantian* (39-2) and then to the left corner. (39-3)

The left palm is facing back, higher than the head, *Hegu* is open, with a little curl in the elbow.

The right hand faces the chest with the middle finger facing the underarm in the middle pointing to the *Jiquan* point (HT 1). The weight is on the left leg with the right heel up.

Look at the right hand and shake down to the lower *Dantian* (39-4), to the right corner.

The right arm is extended to the right and the hand is higher than the head, the right palm is facing back. The left hand faces the chest with the middle finger facing the underarm, by the *Jiquan* (HT 1) point. The weight is on the right leg, with the back heel up (39-5).

Shift your weight again; bring shaking hands to the lower *Dantian*, (39-6) then up to the left side. (39-7) Be sure not to straighten the elbow.

Note: The entire movement is done 2 times to the left, once to the right, all without stopping.

The hands and arms flutter throughout.

Be sure not to straighten the outside arm; the elbow should be slightly bent.

Form 40: Drink Water (3 times) 飲水（三次）

At the end of the 3rd time shaking, move the hands to the front at shoulder height, still shaking. The arms should be shoulder wide (40-1).

Step forward with the left foot, *Yongquan* and toes touch the floor. Keep the weight on the right leg. Bring *Hegu* of both hands to mouth while still shaking (40-2).

Keep shaking *Hegu* down to *Dabao* (40-3),

down to *Huantiao* (40-4),

down both legs, to the knees,

down left lower leg, (40-5),

then back up to the mouth while straightening up the body (40-2).

Repeat this for 2 more times (for a total of 3 times), and continue shaking throughout.

The Drinking Water movement circulates Qi through the gallbladder meridians along the sides of the body.

Dayan Qigong
64 Movements: Specific Instructions

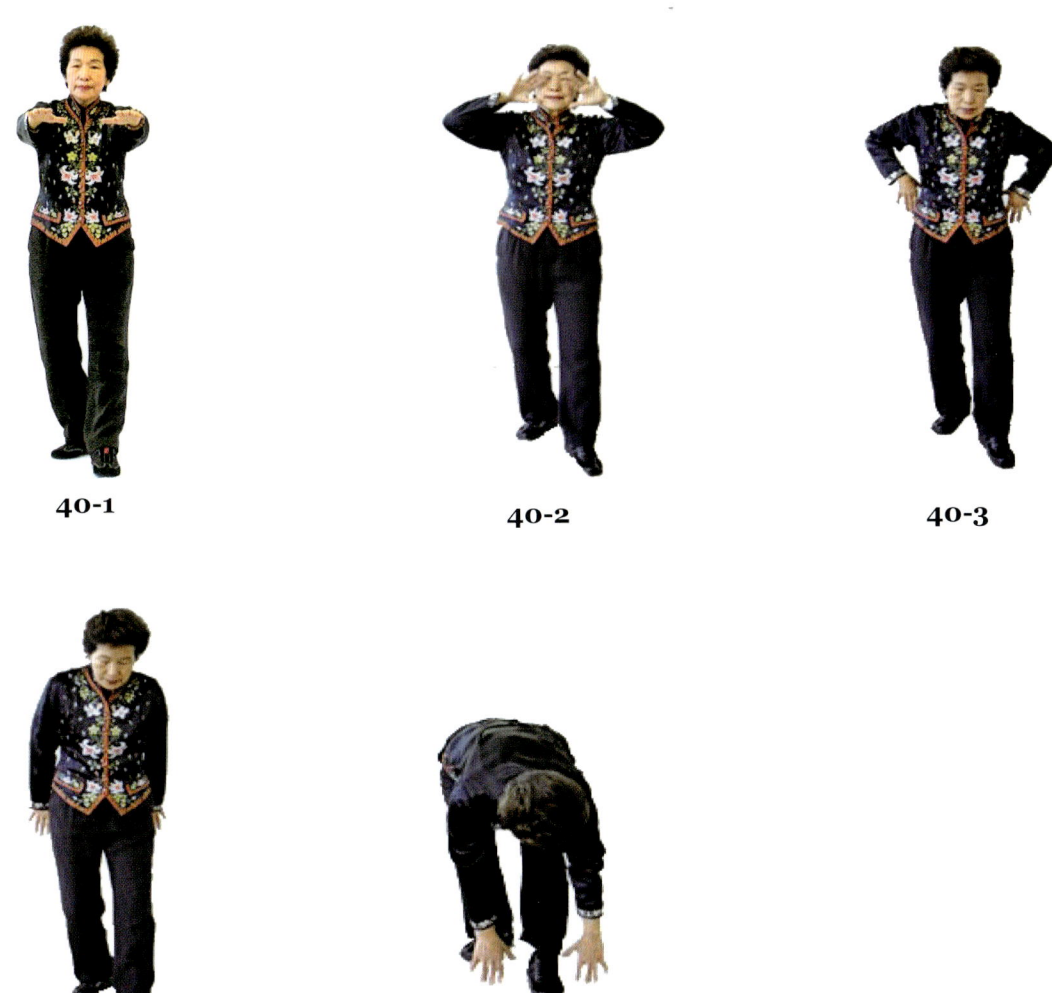

40-1   40-2   40-3

40-4   40-5

Dayan Qigong
64 Movements: Specific Instructions

Form 41: Look at Sky 望天

41-1

41-2

At the end of the 3rd drink water movement, shake the hands to shoulder high, and then bring the right foot forward parallel with the left foot. Stand up straight (41-1), with weight distributed evenly.

Keep shaking the hands up to the sky, and the eyes follow both hands, looking at the sky (41-2).

Form 42: Restore Qi 歸氣

42-1

Continue shaking both hands to the sides of the body, and eyes looking straight ahead.

Shake the hands down and put both hands on both sides of the lower *Dantian*.

The left hand should have all fingers open with the middle finger resting above the naval.

The right hand has all the fingers closed with the thumb open. The index finger touches below the navel. All fingers and palms touch the body (42-1).

Now, both hands shake the stomach to give energy to the stomach – first shake 3 seconds, then stop and stay for 3 seconds, then repeat for 2 more times. After shaking the 3rd time, hold still for 3 seconds.

During the movement, look straight ahead.

NOTE: If having liver problems, reverse the position of the hands, keeping the fingers of the right hand closed with the thumb open, place the right hand with the middle finger touching above the navel. Keep the fingers of the left hand open; the index finger is below the navel.

Form 43: Grasp Qi 抓氣

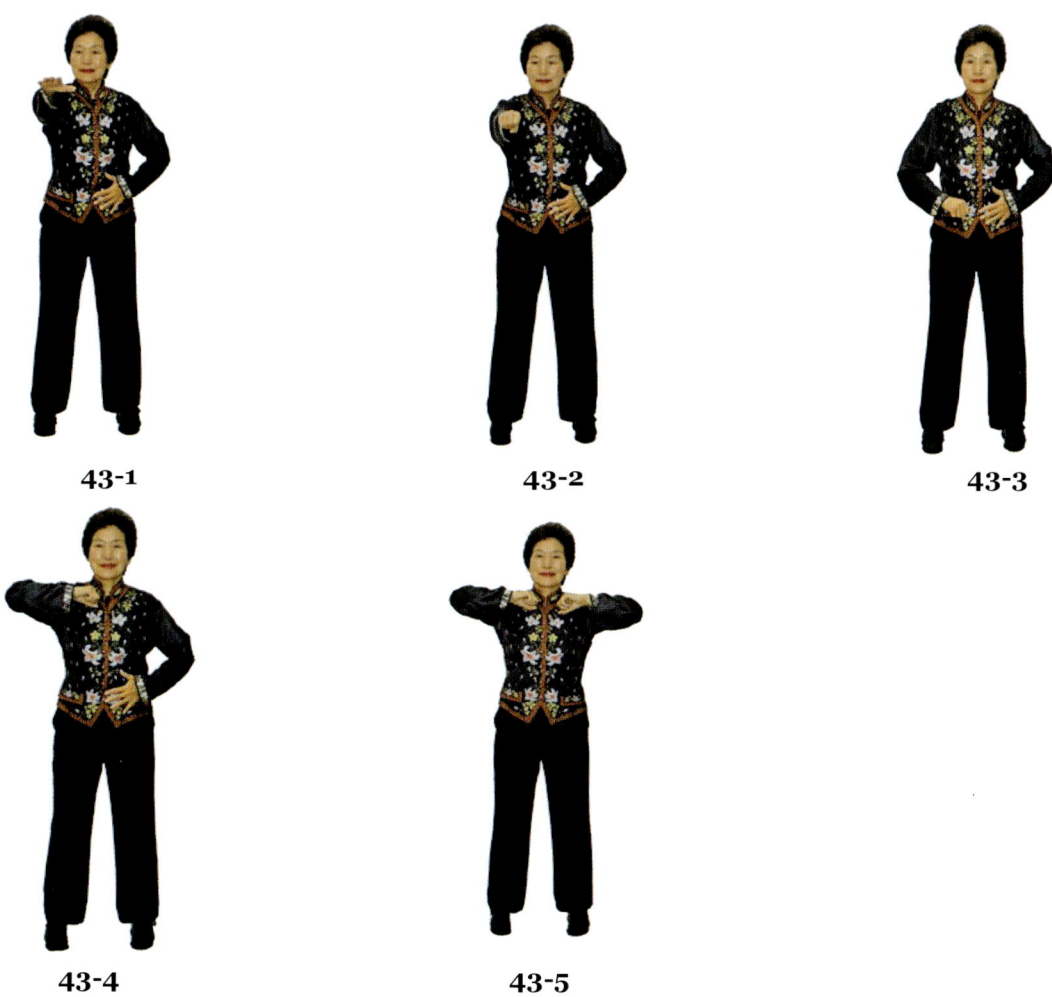

43-1 43-2 43-3

43-4 43-5

Open the fingers of the right hand and move it up the front of the body to *Qihu* high. Extend the hand straight out in front (43-1).
Look at hand.

Close the right hand fingers, with the thumb touching the 1st joint of the middle finger to make an empty fist (43-2).

Dayan Qigong
64 Movements: Specific Instructions

Circle the empty fist down to the lower *Dantian* (43-3) and back to the *Qihu*, placing the hole of the thumb side on the *Qihu* (43-4).

Now the left hand comes up to the *Qihu*, then goes out straight with the fingers extended. Look at the left hand.

Close the fingers of the left hand to make an empty fist, circle the empty fist down to the lower *Dantian*, then up to *Qihu*, placing the hole of the thumb side on *Qihu* (43-5).

Look at the hand each time as it comes out and makes an empty fist, then as the hand returns to the *Qihu*, look straight ahead.

Do these movements back and forth with the right hand and left hand 5 times on each side.

Form 44: Grasp Qi (Palms Up) 翻掌撈氣

44-1  **44-2**  **44-3**

44-4  **44-5**  **44-6**

Open the fingers of the right hand, turn the little fingers towards the *Qihu* (44-1), then the little finger follows the stomach meridian down to the lower *Dantian* (44-2).

Then extend the right hand out *Qihu* high, grasp the Qi by making an empty fist (the thumb is on the middle finger's first joint) (44-3). Bring the right arm back to the body, placing the hole of little finger side on the *Qihu* (44-4).

The left hand turns from the *Qihu*, little finger following the stomach meridian down to the lower *Dantian* (44-5), then circle out to *Qihu* high, make an empty fist, and bring the hand straight into the *Qihu*.

Place the hole of the little finger side on the *Qihu* (44-6).

Dayan Qigong
64 Movements: Specific Instructions

Continue to look at the hand which is out, then when bring up to *Qihu*, look straight. Again, go back and forth with the right and left hand for 5 times on each side, for a total of 10 times.

Form 45: Hold the Ball 抱球

45-1

45-2

45-3

45-4

45-5

Open the fingers of both hands and point the fingers upward. The back of the hands face each other (45-1). At the same time, look at both hands and bring the hands up to the face.

When the hands pass the upper *Dantian*, rotate the hands so the palms are facing the upper *Dantian* (45-2).

Dayan Qigong
64 Movements: Specific Instructions

Keep the hands up and reach up into the sky while turning the hands to have palm facing palm (45-3), looking at the sky.

Then the arms start to open (45-4), turn arms to the sides, then bend the body down.

Move hands closer, finger-to-fingers, about one and a half foot far.

Bend elbows like the two arms are holding a big ball, looking at both hands. (45-5)

Form 46: Massage the Ball 揉球

46-1

46-2

46-3

46-4

Turn the body to the left side (46-1), raise the body higher and bring the palms closer to each other about 9 inches apart, as if holding a ball. Look at both hands.

Dayan Qigong
64 Movements: Specific Instructions

Slowly rotate the hands so the right hand is now above the left hand, palm facing palm about 9 inches apart. The middle of the hands is at the height of the lower *Dantian*, with the fingers spread, and legs straight (46-2).

To massage the ball, make circles turning both hands at the same time to the lower *Dantian*'s direction (46-3). The thumb of the right hand and the little finger of the left hand lead the movement towards the body.

The fingers, wrist, elbows, shoulders, and legs are all moving in the same direction to the right side of the body

Massage the ball or rotate hands 10 times while turning the body to the right side.

After the 5th circle, start bending the left knee and straightening out the right leg and continue to rotate the ball to the right. The whole body moves during this movement. (46-4).

Form 47: Turn and Massage the Ball 轉身揉球

47-1

47-2

47-3

Dayan Qigong
64 Movements: Specific Instructions

47-4

After the 10th rotation to the right side, slowly turn the hands over so that the left hand is on top (47-1). Now the left thumb and the right little finger lead the movement towards the body.

Make circles to massage the ball 8 times to the left side. When the body returns to the middle after the 4th circle, the weight is starting to shift by bending the right knee and straightening the left leg. When reaching the left side after 8 rotations, the weight is shifting again by straightening the left leg and the right leg is bent (47-2).

Do 2 massages back to forward (47-3).

Stand the body straight up and move both hands holding the ball closer to the lower *Dantian*, looking forward. Then open both hands and bring the palms to face the lower *Dantian* (47-4), one inch away.

Form 48: Hold the Qi 抱氣

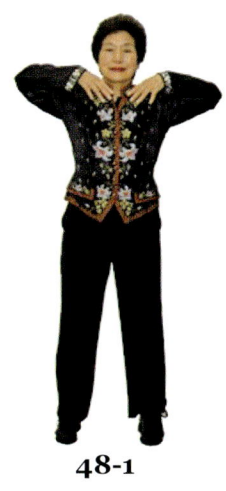
48-1

48-2

48-3

Dayan Qigong
64 Movements: Specific Instructions

48-4

48-5

Relax the fingers and drop them down.

Bring the hands up following the Ren meridian (48-1) to the sky (48-2).

Look at the sky, and arms start to open. (48-3)

Bend down at the hips and bring the hands down to the feet. The hands are a little further from the sides of the feet with the fingers dropped down at the sides of the toes. Look at both hands, and then turn both palms up a little (48-4).

Hold up the ball by bending the knees, and raising the body into a semi sitting position (48-5).

This is meditation. Hands are a little more than shoulder width apart and shoulder height. The back is straight, the neck is straight, the *Baihui* points to the sky and the knees are bent. The fingers are open and a little curl is on the elbows, looking forward.

Relax the body.

Stand in this position for 10 to 15 seconds (or longer for meditation purposes.)

Form 49: Penetrate Qi 貫氣

49-1

49-2

49-3

Stand up, at the same time, the hands hold the Qi and give to the upper *Dantian*, looking forward, thinking about the area of the upper *Dantian*. (49-1)

Move the hands down to the middle *Dantian*, thinking about the area of the middle *Dantian*.

Move the hands down to the lower *Dantian*. Hold at the lower *Dantian* for 3 seconds (49-2).

Continue to lower the hands all the way down, *Laogong* points are facing to the *Huantiao* point. Eyes are looking forward. (49-3)

Form 50: Raise Arms 抬膀

50-1　　　　　　　　　　50-2　　　　　　　　　　50-3

Turn hands so *Hegu* points are facing *Huantiao* points.
Bring hands forward up to shoulder height, looking at hands. (50-1)

Bring the hands back towards the face so the *Hegu*'s are placed next to the mouth. At the same time bring the heels up. (50-2)

Quickly push straight out with hands from the mouth. Heels come down at the same time.

The hands form a triangle with the index fingers 1 inch apart, and the thumbs 2 inches apart. (50-3)

Dayan Qigong
64 Movements: Specific Instructions

Form 51: Turn Wings 翻翅

51-1

51-2

Rotate the hands so the fingers are pointing straight up (51-1) and then drop the fingers down and form them into the claw (51-2).

Form 52: Put the Wings on the Back 背翅

52-1

52-2

Lower the arms and bring the fingers, (still in the claw) down past the *Huantiao* to the kidneys. (52-1)

Place the *Hegu*'s on the kidneys with the palms facing up. Relax the fingers, keeping the fingers pointing up. (52-2)

Shake the *Hegu*'s on the kidneys for 3 seconds, then rest for 3 seconds, then shake again for 3 seconds for a total of 3 times.

Dayan Qigong
64 Movements: Specific Instructions

Form 53: Fly Up (7 times) 起扇上飛（七次）

53-1

53-2

53-3

53-4

53-5

53-6

Dayan Qigong
64 Movements: Specific Instructions

53-7

53-8

53-9

Bring the hands straight down from the kidneys, then up to the front, shoulder height, shoulder width apart. (53-1)

Shift weight to the right foot, moving the right heel in slightly, move the right palm to the lower *Dantian*, and look at the left hand. (53-2)

Step forward with the left foot, *Yongquan* side touching the floor. There is no weight on the front leg.

The left hand comes up and the *Laogong* is facing the upper *Dantian*, and the fingers drop down and are relaxed (53-3).

Look at the left hand and turn at the waist to the left about 30° to 45°.

The left arm opens and reaches outward, with the palm facing the body, make a half circle holding the Qi and give it to the lower *Dantian* (53-4).

Towards the end of the half circle, take the eyes off the left hand and look forward, but still concentrating on the left hand and the lower *Dantian* while moving the left palm to the lower *Dantian*.

Now both palms are at the lower *Dantian*, with the left hand over the right hand (53-5).

Shift the weight to the left leg and step up on the right foot, with the *Yongquan* side touching the floor. Note: when shifting weight to the front foot, the front heel turns inward—in effect "massaging" the *Yongquan* point. Be mindful of balance when changing from one leg to the other.

The right fingers drop down and follow the Ren meridian straight up
(53-6) until the *Laogong* is facing the upper *Dantian*. Look at the right hand (53-7).

Turn at the waist to the right 30º to 45º
(53-8)

The right arm opens and make a half circle to bring the Qi back to the lower *Dantian*. Towards the end of the half circle, take the eyes off the right hand and look forward, but still concentrating on the right hand and the lower *Dantian*.

Repeat the left side again (53-9) for a total of 7 times.

Finish on the left side.

Form 54: Turn Around 轉身

At the last (7th) step, as the left hand is lowered to within one foot of the lower *Dantian*, move the right hand to meet the left hand at the lower *Dantian* about one foot far in front of the *Dantian* (54-1).

Look at both hands and start shaking the hands and arms, put the left heel down, and turn on both heels to the back 180º.

When turning the body, keep shaking the hands and keep the hands about one foot from the lower *Dantian*.

54-1

Dayan Qigong
64 Movements: Specific Instructions

Form 55: Fly Up 飛上

55-1 55-2 55-3

Keep looking at both hands, shaking hands up to point at the sky with the arms parallel.

The weight is on the left leg and the right heel is up. Then separate the arms out to the sides (55-1) and sweep the hands to the sides to between the middle and lower *Dantian*s. (55-2)

Keep shaking the hands and bring them up to shoulder height. (55-3)

Form 56: Fly Over Water (7 times) 過水飛翔（七次）

56-1 56-2 56-3 56-4

Dayan Qigong
64 Movements: Specific Instructions

56-5

56-6

56-7

Looking at left hand step forward with the left leg. This time the *Yongquan* point and the toes are flat on the ground, with the heel up.

Look at the left hand and shake both hands down to knees.

Left palm faces the left knee, right palm faces the right knee, (56-1), and then shake the hands to the left side. Straighten up the body.

The left hand and palm are back, thumb is pointing down, a little curl on the elbow and the left hand is higher than the head.

The right hands', middle finger is facing, and pointing, to the middle of the underarm, at the heart point. Keep shaking the hands and look at the left hand (56-2).

Now shift the weight to the left leg, the left heel turns inward causing the *Yongquan* point to be "massaged." The left heel then touches the ground. Look at the right hand. Take a 2nd step forward with the right leg. The *Yongquan* and toes are touching the ground.

Bend at the waist and shake the hands down to the left knee (56-3 through 56-5), then to the right knee and up to the right side. Continue to look at the right hand (56-6)

The right hand is higher than the head, curl in the elbow, palm facing to the back, thumb is down. The left hand's, middle finger is facing the underarm. (56-6)

Looking at left hand, take a 3rd step forward with the left leg. (The right heel turns inward, "massaging" the right *Yongquan*. The right heel then touches the ground). The *Yongquan* touches on the ground with the heel up.

Look at the left hand and shake both hands down to knees (56-7), bend at the waist, then go to the left side. Repeat this movement for a total of 7 times.

Form 57: Turn Around 轉身

57-1

From the last (7th) step, look at the right hand and shake both hands down to the lower *Dantian*. Flutter both hands in front of the lower *Dantian* about one foot away from the body.

Put the left heel down and turn on both heels to the back 180°. When turning the body, keep shaking the hands and keep the hands about one foot from the lower *Dantian* (57-1).

Same as Forms 54 and 55.

Dayan Qigong
64 Movements: Specific Instructions

Form 58: Fly Up 飛上

58-1   58-2   58-3   58-4

Keep looking at both hands, while shaking them upwards to point to the sky (58-1). The weight is on the left leg and the right heel is up.

Open the arms upwards to the sides (58-2).

Then sweep the hands down and forward to between the middle and lower *Dantian* (58-3).

Keep shaking up to shoulder height (58-4)

Dayan Qigong
64 Movements: Specific Instructions

Form 59: Searching for Food (7 times) 尋食(七次)

59-1    **59-2**    **59-3**

59-4    **59-5**    **59-6**

Stop shaking the hands. The arms open to the sides, lower than the shoulders, close the fingers into the claw hand. Step out with the left foot 30° diagonally to the left corner at 30°. Still the *Yongquan* and toes touch the ground with no weight on the forward leg (59-1).

Open the hands, bend at the waist, and drop down quickly so the arms cross over the forward leg. The left arm is always on top of the right arm. The left palm is facing the right knee and the right palm is facing back. (59-2)

Look at both hands. The *Baihui* faces forward (59-2).

Uncross the arms, with the hands passing in front of the knees (59-3), pulling the hands aside slowly, using the little finger side as you stand up, as if pulling taffy or silk.

The claws form again as the arms are extended to the sides (59-4).

Turn on the left *Yongquan* (left heel turns outward, "massaging" the left *Yongquan,* and then the left heel touches the ground), as the right leg points diagonally 30° to the right corner. No weight is on this leg. At the same time, the arms open to the sides and fingers closed into claws. (59-5)

Open the hands and drop down quickly over the right knee (59-6). The right palm is facing the left knee and the left palm is facing back.

Again, push out pass both knees, straighten up the body, close fingers into the claw, turn on the right *Yongquan* (right heel turns outward, "massaging" the right *Yongquan* and then the right heel touches the ground), and take a step diagonally 30° with the left leg.

Do this for 7 times dropping down quickly and pulling the hands aside slowly. Start with the left side and end with the left side.

Form 60: Turn Around 轉身

60-1

60-2

60-3

After the 7th time of Searching for Food, bring both hands to each knee (60-1).

Dayan Qigong
64 Movements: Specific Instructions

Bring the hands up the legs to the lower *Dantian* (60-2), and keep the hands at the lower *Dantian*. The elbows are still curled.

Put left heel down. Turn on the left heel, then right heel to face 180° toward the opposite direction (60-3).

Form 61: Seeking Nest (7 Movements) 尋窩 (左, 中, 右, 右, 中, 左, 中)

For movement 61, the 7 steps can be broken down as follows:

Step	Front leg is...	Body is Facing...	Picture number
1	Left	Left	61-1 and 61-2
2	Right	Center	61-3 and 61-4
3	Left	Right	61-5
4	Right	Right	61-6
5	Left	Center	61-7
6	Right	Left	61-8
7	Left	Center	61-9 (same as 61-7)

61-1   61-2   61-3

Dayan Qigong
64 Movements: Specific Instructions

61-4  **61-5**  **61-6**

61-7  **61-8**  **61-9**

Keep the hands at the lower *Dantian* and turn the hands horizontally. Take the 1st step with the left foot; the *Yongquan* and toes touch the ground with no weight on the left leg. Turn the body to the left 90°, at the same time scan the horizon (61-1 and 61-2).

Bring the hands up just below the middle *Dantian*. Point the finger tips to finger tips, look at the hands, bring them up slightly to the middle *Dantian*, and push down with the palms and wrists to just below the waist (61-2). When pushing down, go as low as the curl on the elbows will take and keeping the elbows curled.

After pushing down, relax the fingers and point them downward, then raise the hands to the Dai meridian with both *Laogong* points facing to the Dai meridian.

Dayan Qigong
64 Movements: Specific Instructions

Now look forward and turn the body to the center, scanning the horizon with the eyes while turning. Take a 2nd step forward with the right foot (61-3).

Raise the hands slightly, point the fingers to fingers, and then push down to below the waist, looking at the hands while pushing down (61-4).

Now relax and drop the fingers down, and look forward. Take a 3rd step forward with the left leg. Turn the body to the right 90° and scan the horizon with the eyes.

Bring the hands up a little, and then push down with the finger tips to finger tips (61-5)

Take a 4th step forward with the right leg. This time stay on the right side and repeat coming up and pushing down movements with the hands (61-6).

Now relax and drop the fingers down, and look forward. Turn the body to the center and scan the horizon with the eyes.

Take a 5th step forward with the left leg. Facing forward, bring the hands up and then push down to the front while looking at the hands (61-7).

Now relax and drop the fingers down. Take a 6th step forward with the right leg. Turn the body to the left 90° and scan the horizon with the eyes. Pushing down to the left while looking at the hands (61-8).

Now relax and drop the fingers down, and look forward. Turn the body to the center and scan the horizon with the eyes.

Finally take the last (7th) step forward with the left leg. Facing forward, bring the hands up and then push down to the front while looking at the hands (61-9).

Note: When transitioning your weight, the front *Yongquan* is "massaged," the heel turns inward and then touches the ground. After that, the back leg goes forward.

Master Liu in Taiwan practicing with students

Form 62: Turn and Swim 轉身泳動

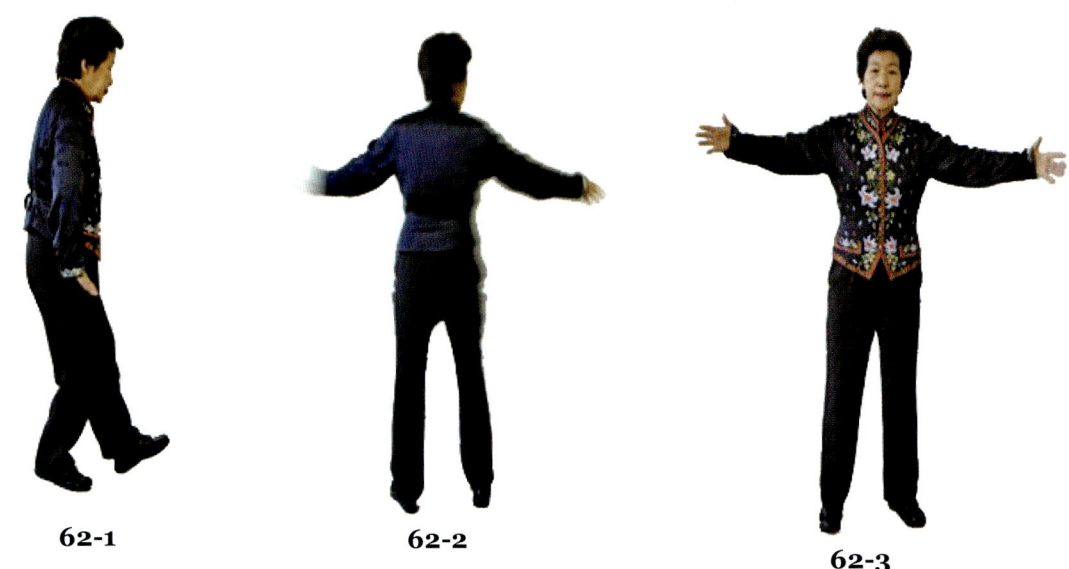

62-1 **62-2** **62-3**

After the last push down, turn on the left heel 90° to the left (62-1). Now the body is facing the original direction at the beginning of this set.

Bring the hands down to the side, and start shaking them.

The right foot comes up and stand parallel to the left foot, at shoulder width apart. Raise up both heels.

The body is now facing in the original direction when started the 1st movement of the set.

Keeping the hands open as they continue shaking to the sides of the body (62-2 and 62-3).

Dayan Qigong
64 Movements: Specific Instructions

Form 63: Sleep Peacefully and Restore Qi 安睡歸氣

63-1

63-2

63-3

63-4

63-5

63-6

63-7

Continue shaking the hands, bringing both arms up to give Qi to the upper *Dantian*. (63-1)

Continue shaking and giving Qi to the middle *Dantian*.

Stop shaking at the middle *Dantian*, and bring the fingers together. (63-2)

Bring hands down to the lower *Dantian*.

All the fingers are closed and the thumbs pointing up towards the head.

The fingers and palms touch the body. The middle fingers touch the sides of the navel, and the thumbs are pointing towards ST18 (*Rugen*) points. (63-3)

Both heels are still up off the floor (63-4)

Squat down keeping both hands on the lower *Dantian*, elbows relaxed and to the sides. (63-5)

The eyes are looking down toward the floor and the *Baihui* point is straight ahead.

Heels are up, and the knees are pointing straight forward.

The body is situated so the back and neck are as straight as possible, and the relaxed elbows are in the middle of the body. (63-6)

New students should keep their eyes open. After practicing for one month, then close the eyes after squatting down. Stay in this position for 10 to 15 seconds.

Dayan Qigong
64 Movements: Specific Instructions

Form 64: Closing Form 收式

64-1

64-2

64-3

64-4

64-5

64-6

64-7

Open eyes, bring head up, heels down, and then stand straight up. (64-1)
Looking forward, open the fingers and come down following the Ren meridian, (64-2).

Now open the hands to the sides, and making the final close of the form (64-3).

Hold the Qi to the top of the upper *Dantian*, sinking into the upper *Dantian*, (64-4) down to the middle *Dantian*, sinking into the middle *Dantian*, down to the lower *Dantian* (64-5), and then all the way down, bringing the Qi all the way down (64-6).

Move arms to the side of the body and bring legs together (64-7). Either leg can move to close with the other leg. Stay in this position for a few seconds. Let the Qi work on the body.

Dayan Qigong
64 Movements: Specific Instructions

Walking Meditation 行功

Walk normally gathering the Qi with the hand opposite to the extended leg and bring it to the lower *Dantian*.

Take another step and gather Qi from the other hand opposite the extended leg and give to the lower *Dantian*. (A, B)

Continue to walk slowly and concentrate on the lower *Dantian*

Remember when doing Qigong, always keep the body relaxed and the mind clear.

A

B

Dayan Qigong
Hand and Foot Positions

Hand and Foot Positions

In Dayan Qigong the hand and foot positions are used to bring qi to the body or to expel or release it from the body. Qi sensation is usually felt first and most strongly in the hands. The basic hand and foot positions and their functions are listed below.

Naturally Open Shape

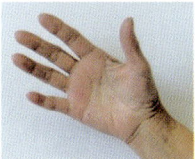

The hand is completely open, thumb slightly curved, the other fingers straight but not rigid, fingers slightly apart. This position enables the qi in the hand meridians to move freely to the fingers and to connect the qi in each finger.

Spoon Shape

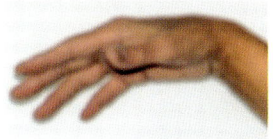

The palm is curved inward and the back of the hand is also curved. The fingers are relaxed and slightly apart, and the wrist is bent inward or downward. This position helps to bring qi to the *Laogong* points.

Empty Fist

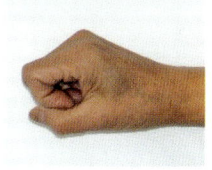 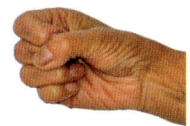

The four fingers are curled inward, tips touching the palm. The thumb is curved over the top of the middle finger at the first joint. The fist is not clenched, there is a space between the fingers and the palm, and the muscles are relaxed. This form is to bring the qi to the body

Pursed hand (Plum Blossom Hand)

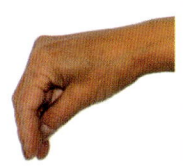 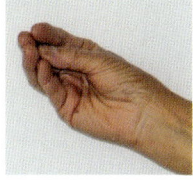

The five fingers are naturally curved together, thumb touching the inside first joint of the middle finger. This position is for gathering the qi to the five fingers and bringing it to certain points on the body.

Pushing With Hands

The palms are facing outward with the hand curved upward from the wrist. The four fingers of each hand are straight, but not stiff. The thumb is curved slightly toward the fingers, and there is a curve between the thumb and the index finger.

Dayan Qigong
Hand and Foot Positions

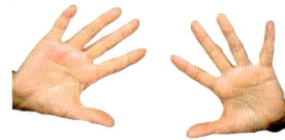 This shape can expel qi from the fingers, palm, and wrist. If when using this shape, the 10 fingers are facing each other, with both elbows slightly curved outward, you will feel a very strong qi sensation.

Note: When the palms face up the qi is raised, and when the palms face down, the qi is lowered or pushed down.

Shaking Arms

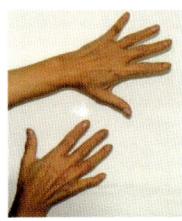 Arms are extended, naturally straight but not rigid, and wrists are relaxed. From the wrists, shake arms, hands and fingers with small rapid fluttering movements. This hand movement increases circulation of blood, delivers qi into the meridians, and expels disease qi.

Parallel Foot Position

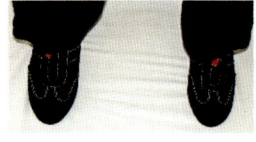 Standing with feet parallel and shoulder - width apart. This balances yin and yang and centers the mind and the body. With equal pressure on both feet, the qi in the three yin and three yang foot meridians is also balanced.

Empty Heel

 In this position, either the toe is on the ground and the heel is raised, or the outside of the *Yongquan* is the only part of the foot touching the ground. The rest of the foot remains "empty". This serves to open the *Yongquan* point on the bottom of the foot and to bring qi to it. It also aids in bringing qi to the foot meridians.

Landing Heel

 The heels are brought up and then landed on the ground abruptly – the heels going powerfully from empty to solid. This is to wake up the internal yang qi, raise the qi in the three yin meridians, and bring qi down in the three yang meridians of the legs. Bad qi is thus expelled from the legs and the feet.

Dayan Qigong
Major Points

The following are the major points which are most used in Dayan Qigong set. The letters and numbers refer to the meridian location of each point.

Please look at the point charts for a more exact location of each. These points are explained in a way that is easy to understand for the readers.

Hegu (LI 4)
合谷穴
At the V formed by the bones of the thumb and forefinger of both hands. About ½ inch above the V form on top of the hands.

Shenshu (BL 23)
腎俞穴
On either side of the spine just above the waist at the kidneys.

Laogong (PC 8)
勞宮穴
In the center of the palms on both hands.

Baihui (GV 20)
百會穴
On top of the head in the center on a line directly up from the tips of the ears.

Quepen (ST 12)
缺盆穴
Above the center of the collarbone on both sides.

Yongquan (K 1)
湧泉穴
On the soles of the feet in the center behind the ball of the foot.

Huantiao (GB 30)
環跳穴
In the hollow of the hip on the buttocks on both sides.

Qihu (ST 13)
氣戶穴
Beneath the collarbone directly below the *Quepen* points on both sides.

Yintang (Ex 2)
印堂穴
Between the eyebrows. Also known as Upper (Shang) *Dantian*.

Taiyang (Ex 5)
太陽穴
Between the outer canthus of the eyes and the temple on each side of the head.

Sanyinjiao (SP 6)
三陰交穴
Three cuns above the point of the ankle bone on the inside of the leg on both sides.

Jiquan (HT 1)
極泉穴
In the center of each armpit.

Dayan Qigong
Major Points

Rugen (ST 18)
乳根
In the 5th intercostal space, below the nipple, 4 cun lateral to the anterior midline.

Dabao (SP 21)
大包穴
On the lateral side of the chest and on the middle axillary line, in the 7th intercostal space.

Liangqiu (ST 34)
梁丘穴
2 cun above the laterosuperior border of the knee cap.

Shang Dantian
上丹田
Upper *Dantian*. On the forehead, midway of the line connecting both eyebrows.

Zhong Dantian
中丹田
Middle *Dantian*. In the chest, midway between the nipples.

Xia Dantian
下丹田
Lower *Dantian*. In the abdomen, 1½ inches behind the umbilicus.

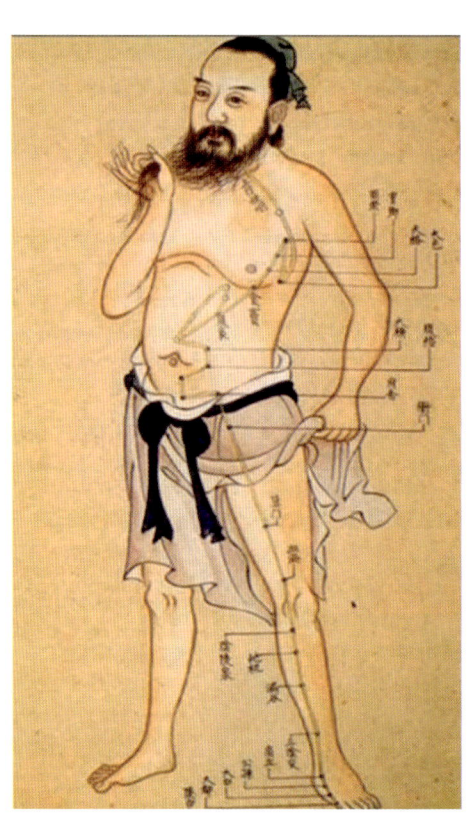

Dayan Qigong
Meditation

Dayan Qigong includes both an active practice and a quiet or meditative, practice. Both are essential and should be done each day. The active practice is not simply a muscular and aerobic exercise, but the movement of the Qi throughout the meridians. This movement of Qi strengthens the organs, blood, nerves and meridians, and exercises and strengthens the ligaments, tendons, bones, skin, and muscles. It is, therefore, both an internal and external exercise.

Dayan Qigong meditation is different from other kinds of meditation in several ways. In this form of meditation it is necessary that your hand be placed on the *Liangqiu* points (St 34), thumbs on the *Xuehai* points (SP 10). These points are located adjacent to the knees, which are particularly important, because it is here that the Qi of several meridians converge. By placing the hands as described, the Qi is sent to all meridians during meditation.

Placing the thumbs on the *Xuehai* points is important for blood circulation and blood production, and may help certain blood diseases. Some say that this particular position can also be helpful in alleviating menstrual problems, lumbar pain, leg paralysis, and uterine spasms. Sitting in this position can prevent numbness of legs and feet during long practice sessions.

The principle in the meditation practice is movement in quiet. Even as you sit completely still, calming the body and the mind, the Qi is moving through the meridians and the internal organs.

The quiet practice increases the speed of the circulation of Qi through what is known as the Zhou Tian. Like Qi, the words "Zhou Tian" describes both a thing (in this case a place or location on the body) and a function. Zhou Tian refers both to the circulation of energy through a closed circular path and to the circular path itself.

There are two aspects of Zhou Tian – large (Da Zhou Tian) and small (Xiao Zhou Tian). One of the most important effects of long-term practice is the movement of Qi through the Zhou Tian. As you advance, you will notice this flow, manifested usually as heat, traveling up the midline of the back, neck, and head through what is known as the Du channel and down the middle of the front of the upper body - the Ren channel. Occasionally this energy flow is reversed, going up the Ren channel and down the Du channel. The reason for keeping the tongue on the roof of the mouth during both the quiet and active practices of Dayan Qigong is to connect the two channels.

The Du and Ren channels constitute the Xiao Zhou Tian. The Da Zhou Tian consists of the Du and Ren channels, twelve regular meridians plus the eight extraordinary channels – those not connected directly to organs. The movement of Qi through the Xiao and Da Zhou Tian brings it to the entire body.

Dayan Qigong
Meditation

During meditation, keep your mind calm and peaceful, clear and peaceful, clear and free of any thoughts. If such thoughts or images arise as you sit, just let them go and focus, temporarily, on the lower *Dantian* or the *Yongquan* points (K 1).

There are two techniques for sitting, and we will explain both.

The Natural Sinking Qi Technique 自然沉氣法

Sitting should be done in a quiet and comfortable environment that is free from distractions. Sit about two inches onto the chair or bench so that the *Huiyin* point (CV 1) is just off the edge of the chair.

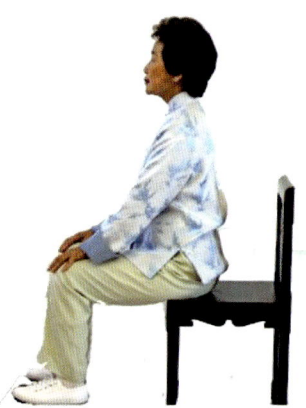

The upper body and thighs should be at 90º (degrees) relation to each other, and the legs should form 90º (degrees) angle with the floor.

The distance between the feet should equal the distance between the shoulders.

You can also choose to sit cross-legged on the floor. Women should cross the left leg in front of the right, and men with the right leg in front.

In either case, the tongue should be lightly touching the palate just behind the front teeth, and the back teeth should be touching, but not clenched. The lips are lightly closed. The whole body should be relaxed, and breathing should be natural.

To begin, use both hands to carry Qi from the universe and bring it to the top of the head. Slowly bring your hands down to the upper *Dantian*, then down and pass the tip of the nose, then down the *Ren* meridian to the middle *Dantian* (right before which point your eyes will be lightly closed), and then down to the lower *Dantian*, 1.5 inches behind the navel.

Dayan Qigong
Meditation

Upper body and legs at 90°　　Both hands carry Qi from the Universe　　Bring this Qi to the upper *Dantian*

   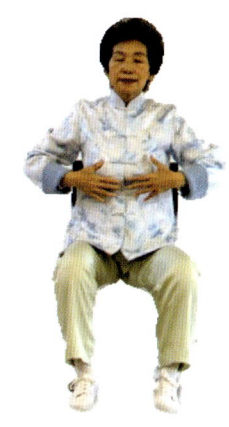   

As hands pass the nose　　Contemplate the middle *Dantian*　　Palms on *Liangqiu*, thumbs on *Xuehai* points

Continue the contemplation down the *Ren* meridian to the *Huiyin* point (REN 1). Place the center of the palms of both hands (the *Laogong* points) on the *Liangqiu* points located near the kneecaps, thumbs lightly touching the *Xuehai* points.

During meditation, keep your mind calm and peaceful, clear and free of any unnecessary thoughts. If such thoughts or images arise as you sit, just let them go and briefly focus on the lower *Dantian*.

When finishing the meditation, keep the eyes closed, rub the palms of the hands together for 7 times. Then rub the eyeballs, with the eyes closed for 7 times. The right hand go in a clockwise direction while the left hand go in counterclockwise direction. Rub the eyes with the little finger side of the palm.

Dayan Qigong
Meditation

With the eyes still closed, wash face and comb hair with hands starting from under the chin, come up with the hands touching the face or 1 to 2 inches away, to the top of the head, around the head to the front of the chin for 6 times. After the 6th time, slowly open the eyes, and finish wash face, comb hair for the 7th time while the eyes slowly open.

Do a final close, giving the Qi to the upper *Dantian*, middle *Dantian*, and lower *Dantian*.

Rub palms together for 7 times   Rub eyeballs for 7 times   Wash face, comb hair

After 6th time slowly open eyes   Wash face, comb hair for 7th time, eyes open   Make final close

There is no specific duration for this meditation practice. For beginners sitting for 10 minutes is enough. Later, gradually increase the sitting times to 30 minutes or longer, as long as you are comfortable.

The Silent Reading Technique 默念法

This technique is particularly useful for beginning students and for those who have difficulty relaxing and calming their minds. Many beginners have trouble concentrating. When they have closed their eyes, thoughts of work, study, relationships, problems, and fantasies fill their minds, thereby reducing the effectiveness of meditation.

If you have trouble concentrating, this silent reading technique should help. Each time your mind begins to wonder, pronounce (silently) the words "Gong Cheng" monotone as many times as necessary. Gong Cheng means to practice successfully, will help to focus the mind. At the end of either form of meditation, rub your hands together 7 times (eyes still closed), then massage your eyes gently 7 times with either the palms or the heels of your hands using a circular motion, thus refreshing the eyes with Qi.

Finally, bring hands to the bottom of the chin, up the front of the face, over to the top of the head, to back of neck, and to front of the chin slowly opening your eyes after the 6th time. Then carry the Qi from the upper to middle to lower *Dantian* as you did when you opened your meditation. Sit quietly for a moment before you get up and move around.

There is no specified duration for this meditation practice. For beginners sitting for 10 minutes is enough. Later, gradually increase the sitting times to 30 minutes or longer, as long as you are comfortable both during and after your meditation.

Remember to always keep your mind clear.

Master Hui Liu meditating on Yellow Mountain, China.

Dayan Qigong
Meditation

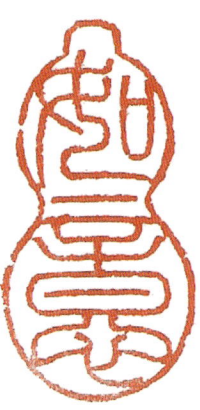

Master Hui Liu's painting of Guan Yin Bodhisattva

Dayan Qigong
Meditation

Mediation and Dayan Qigong

Meikyo Robert Rosenbaum

Master Hui Liu wisely reminds us that Dayan Qigong is not restricted to the 64 movements of the form; all day long we practice within an ongoing flow of qi, within us and all around us. Our relationship to the internal and outer world involves harmonizing and balancing this flow moment by moment. Because of this, meditation is an integral part of Dayan Qigong practice, but people have many mistaken ideas about meditation.

Meditation is not an esoteric mystery nor a harsh discipline. Zen Master Dogen is eloquent about this. In his instructions for *zazen* (Zen seated meditation) he advises us that meditation "is not learning to do concentration. It is the gateway to great ease and joy."

When students learning Dayan Qigong focus only on the movements, they can easily get trapped in fantasies of accomplishment and agonies of frustration and failure. If you practice with a confused mind, you may think you can learn the movements and arrive at some level of mastery. This is a very mechanical view. Qigong is not something one ever masters: it is inexhaustible. Qigong is a lifelong practice that deepens day by day and year by year.

The mind with which you exercise your life is the body of your practice. This mind is limitless, because it is ungraspable. You can become intimate with this mind through meditation. Meditation removes all distractions and insists you find your place where you are. When you find your place where you are, practice occurs.

How you practice is just as or perhaps more important than how *much* you practice. If you practice with a self-centered mind seeking to gain health only for yourself, your qi will turn in on itself and become poisonous. Dayan Qigong teaches us to harmonize self and other, hard and soft, yin and yang for the benefit of all beings. This attitude emerges naturally in meditation.

Because the movements of the qigong form require concentration and attention, strength and flexibility, it is easy to fall into the error of striving too hard, get tired, and then practice too little. For this reason it is important to develop a big mind that serves as a large container. When there is space in mind it steadies your concentration and softens the harsh glare of your self-critical attention; you have room for your thoughts and muscle fibers to be supple and are refreshed with energy for stamina and power. This allows you to cultivate *wu-wei*, a central tenet of Taoist practice. *Wu-wei* is sometimes translated as "effortless effort" or "do not-doing," but these words fall short. When you drop your self-centered concerns and allow the movements to move you, instead of "doing" qigong you merge with the movements: yin and yang flower naturally in selfless generosity.

Dayan Qigong
Meditation

The qigong movements are themselves a moving meditation. They are greatly complemented by sitting meditation. Sitting meditation helps you become intimate with stillness so that, during the 64 movements, you abide in stillness. Sitting meditation allows you to taste how, at the heart of stillness, eternity still flows.

Moment by moment, moving still. When you practice, put aside all involvements and let the myriad things rest. Sitting and lying down, standing and walking, during all your hours, meditation deepens your qigong practice of wonder, gratitude, and joy.

Silent Contemplation painted by Master Hui Liu, 2013

Dayan Qigong
FAQ's

1. Is Dayan Qigong a safe exercise?

As we have stated before, Dayan Qigong is a safe exercise without negative side effects. Those who have had no previous experience with it may find it a bit mystifying at first. You may have heard that doing Qigong incorrectly can create problems. Dayan Qigong, however, is different from other forms in that it is absolutely safe, and even if you do it incorrectly, you cannot harm yourself, though you will not experience its benefits. By practicing correctly and concentrating on the movements, allowing the circulation of both internal and external Qi, you can benefit almost immediately. The combination of movements will bring Qi to all your meridians, balance Yin and Yang in your body, and enhance the circulation of both blood and Qi. All you have to do is relax, concentrate on what you are doing, keep your tongue on your upper palate behind the teeth, and you will unite mind, body, and Qi. No one has ever been known to suffer adversely from the practice of Dayan Qigong.

2. Is it possible to learn Dayan Qigong without a teacher or using an instruction manual?

It is possible to learn Dayan Qigong without a teacher, following diagrams, video tapes, and written explanations, though it is a much less effective way to learn. The diagrams may not be accurate, there is no one to answer any questions you may have, and you are not able to monitor your own mistakes as effectively as an experienced teacher can. However, if you are obliged to learn without a teacher, do only those movements you are completely sure you understand, and practice these over and over, concentrating well. Be sure that you practice for at least ten minutes at a time, since it takes that much time to get the Qi moving and to strengthen the *Dantian*.

3. Why does Dayan Qigong affect health?

In doing Dayan Qigong, you are expelling bad or diseased causing Qi from your body and taking in beneficial Qi from the environment, circulating it through the body. As you progress in your practice, and expel more and more stagnant Qi, beneficial Qi begins to accumulate in the body, enhancing your health. The accumulation process occurs through the gradual opening of the *Laogong* points in the palms of the hands and later of the *Yongquan* points (KI 1) in the feet, and the *Baihui* point (VC 20) on the top of the head. Long years of practicing will eventually enable you to generate your own Qi.

4. Is it possible to do other systems of martial arts while studying Dayan Qigong?

Any martial arts system requires intense concentration. Each system is different and has different points of focus or emphasis. If you are studying a number of systems at one time, it is likely that you will have difficulty concentrating on any of them, and it is probable that you will not be able to learn any one of them adequately.

Beginners are advised, therefore to wait until they have learned the entire Dayan Qigong set before learning another system. Once you have mastered this set and have the time and energy, you will benefit from learning other forms.

You can continue to engage in sports like swimming, running, gymnastics, basketball, tennis, etc.

It is always advisable to do both the active and the meditative styles together in order to strengthen your Qi. If you already know and practice other martial arts, it is always advisable to do Dayan Qigong after rather than before you do these.

5. *Is it advisable to do Dayan Qigong while you have a cold or flu?*
With a high fever, it is best to follow doctor's advice and get plenty of rest, being careful not to exhaust yourself. When the fever subsides or when you are just coming down with an illness, if you have enough energy, Dayan Qigong can be helpful and is recommended.

At the beginning of a cold when you are sneezing and have a runny nose, Dayan Qigong may reduce your symptoms. As you practice you may feel Qi being expelled from the palms of your hands and the center of the soles of the feet. The body may feel hot and sweaty, but you will also feel comfortable and relaxed.

Some people who have been particularly susceptible to colds and flu find that after they have done the set for some time they catch fewer colds, and when they do catch cold their symptoms are less severe.

6. How much time is necessary each day for practicing, and are there special requirements?
The amount of time depends on one's health, living conditions and environments. It is best to practice twice a day, once in the morning and once in the evening, for at least half an hour. The minimum amount of practice should be at least 10 minutes, as this is the time necessary to begin the Qi moving in the body.

There are no special requirements for Dayan Qigong other than common sense measures for any exercise. You are urged to do it correctly for maximum benefit, but even done incorrectly, you cannot do harm to yourself, and you may even experience some positive results. People of any age or physical conditions can do it, and it is very adaptable to individual needs. As you progress in your practice of Dayan Qigong you will notice a more flexible and healthier body, a greater vitality, and calmer and more concentrated mind.

Dayan Qigong
General Considerations

Dayan Qigong moving practice consists of two sets of 64 movements. The first set of 64 movements can be divided into four parts as follows:

Movements 1 through 36 involve the circulation of 12 Yin and Yang meridians. Qi is being taken into the body, activating or increasing energy in the meridians, and bringing the Qi through the whole body; arms and legs, side to side, front and back, inside and outside, head to feet, and then feet to hands.

Movements 37 through 42 involve fluttering the hands, making the Qi flow more strongly in the meridians. These movements mainly rid the body of stagnant Qi.

Movements 43 through 52 involve taking positive Qi into the three *Dantian* areas in the forehead, center of the chest, and around the navel. The Qi feeds the meridians and the major organs.

Movements 53 through 62 involve walking exercise. This is the more active part of the set. The others are more stationary. Combining both the stationary and the active movements make the set more effective.

Movement 63, "Sleeping", brings the Qi to the lower *Dantian*, "returning to the source." The Closing ends the exchange of Qi and return Qi to its meridian..

Thus the entire set goes from Jing (quiet) to Dong (active) to Jing (quiet).

As a beginner, be sure to do the set in a quiet and relaxed manner, and do the movements correctly. Some moves are faster, some are soft, and some are mixed. Keep your body flexible, (The relaxed parts are not to be done loosely, and the tight parts not stiff.) Keep the movement even and smooth and do the set at an even tempo.

Later, when practicing Qigong, the Qi will be felt. Once you feel Qi, only notice it, do not try to direct the flow of Qi to a certain place in the body. Qi sensations may be in various parts of the body, still keep your thoughts on the following movements or on the moment.

If you feel a cold coming on, do the set three times in succession and you will feel better.

It is important to pay attention to where directing the gaze in each movement. Sometimes the gaze looks into the distance and sometimes the gaze is being directed to the hands or at the sky or ground. Each movement will give more detail direction of gaze. This helps to concentrate the Qi in the body.

During the entire set, keep the lips together, the back teeth touching lightly, and gently placing the tip of the tongue on top of the mouth just behind the front teeth. This connects the Ren and Du Channels and permits Qi to flow up the back and down the front of the body, which enhances the connection of the Xiao Zhou Tian.

Dayan Qigong
General Considerations

Generally, unless specified otherwise, the hands and fingers should remain open and relaxed. The fingers should not be touching each other, nor should they be held rigid. Relax the joints a bit so that the fingers curve a little. Be sure also that the thumb is relaxed and curved a bit. This will create a hollow in the palms of the hands and facilitate Qi flowing freely to and from the hands.

In some of the movements, the *Hegu* point between the thumb and forefinger is open. This is done by slightly flexing the thumb and forefinger out so as to create some tension in the space between the two. Opening the *Hegu* point facilitates the flow and connection of Qi.

Many of the movements require bending or stooping. If your physical condition is such that you cannot do these, you can imagine yourself bending. As athletes can maintain their abilities through visualization, you can also achieve benefit from visualizing the movement. Apparently, the body does not differentiate if the concentration is strong enough.

As a beginner, it may help in some of the movements by looking at yourself in a mirror to get the right position. Your muscles do have their own memory of movement, and soon your body will get the feeling of the correct position. Your body will also remember the set no matter what your mind might be doing, and as you advance in your practice you may find your mind wandering considerable. When that happens, realize that this is normal and gently bring your mind back to concentrate on the movement. The more you practice concentrating, the more you will be able to do it. And the less you will find your body and mind widely separated and the less you will find your body dutifully doing the set while your mind is galloping off by itself somewhere in a distance place or time.

Relax your body and pay attention to its moving movements. It might be helpful, particularly as a beginner, occasionally do the set very slowly, noticing areas in your body, which you tense up, especially the shoulders, buttocks, and back. Release the tension when you do notice it. After a while, you will become accustomed to doing the movement without unnecessarily tensing.

Choose a place and time to practice when you are not likely to be disturbed, and try to set it aside as a space in which you will not worry about problems, things that must be done, etc., so that your mind may be as free from distractions as possible. Also, try to find a time each day, which is generally a free interval. Make it a regular event.

It is very important that you do the set regularly in a quiet place when you can achieve the necessary quietness of mind. These days, admittedly, it is difficult, with all the demands on our attention and time, but if you can allow yourself the interval for Qigong, you will find that the quietness and concentration carry over into other areas during the day.

Dayan Qigong
General Considerations

More importantly, the emphasis on doing the set in modern life is not only for your health, but also for enjoyment. It is fairly easy to do, makes you feel good about yourself and your body, and can be more like dancing than working out. It can be a time to recharge yourself and your energy, quiet the infernal chatter of the mind, and allow you to better meet the challenges of the day.

Dayan Qigong standing meditation

Dayan Qigong
Factors that May Affect Qigong Practice

It is important when doing the active practice that the movements are done correctly and attentively, and sitting in the correct position when doing the meditative practice. Do them both regularly and believe in them. Do not force or push yourself to achieve preconceived results. Circulation and strengthening of Qi will happen gradually and spontaneously with regular practice.

Before beginning, be as calm and relaxed as possible. Quiet the mind and get focused. Do not be distracted by intruding thoughts. Dismiss them gently by focusing on the lower *Dantian* or recite "Gong Cheng" silently and return to quieting the mind and focusing.

If you hear something, it should be as though you are not really hearing it, and if you see something, as though you do not recognize it. If something startles you, try not to stop suddenly. If you must stop during the set, first close by gathering the Qi to the *Dantian*, proceeding slowly and calmly from the upper, to middle, then lower *Dantian*.

There are internal states and external factors, which can affect the well-being of the body and should be taken into account. The seven emotional states are joy, anger, melancholy, obsessive thoughts or worry, sadness, fear, and fright or alarm. They govern and in turn are governed by particular organs. All emotions are natural when they are in balance or appropriate; but extreme, unresolved, and long-lasting emotions cause imbalance and sickness. Excessive joy will damage the heart; excessive anger will harm the liver; excessive worry or obsessive thinking will weaken the spleen, excessive melancholy or depression will hurt the stomach; excessive sadness or grief is harmful to the lungs; excessive fear injures the gall bladder; and excessive fright or shock is damaging to the kidneys. You can protect yourself from harm done by these emotions by using Qigong to relax and focus the mind.

Also, try to be aware of externally caused factors which can affect your health such as wind, cold, summer heat, dampness, and dryness. Protect yourself from these by being aware of them and taking measures to compensate for or alleviate them (moving out of a draft, coming in from the cold, adding or removing layers of clothing, etc.). Finally, it is best not to practice during a thunderstorm, since it interferes with one's electric and magnetic fields.

Dayan Qigong
Factors that May Affect Qigong Practice

Dayan Qigong moving practice consists of two sets of 64 movements. The first set of 64 movements can be divided into four parts as follows:

Movements 1 through 36 involve the circulation of 12 Yin and Yang meridians. Qi is being taken into the body, activating or increasing energy in the meridians, and bringing the Qi through the whole body; arms and legs, side to side, front and back, inside and outside, head to feet, and then feet to hands.

Movements 37 through 42 involve fluttering the hands, making the Qi flow more strongly in the meridians. These movements mainly rid the body of stagnant Qi.

Movements 43 through 52 involve taking positive Qi into the three *Dantian* areas in the forehead, center of the chest, and around the navel. The Qi feeds the meridians and the major organs.

Movements 53 through 62 involve walking exercise. This is the more active part of the set. The others are more stationary. Combining both the stationary and the active movements make the set more effective.

Movement 63, "Sleeping", brings the Qi to the lower *Dantian*, "returning to the source." The Closing ends the exchange of Qi and return Qi to its meridian..

Thus the entire set goes from Jing (quiet) to Dong (active) to Jing (quiet).

As a beginner, be sure to do the set in a quiet and relaxed manner, and do the movements correctly. Some moves are faster, some are soft, and some are mixed. Keep your body flexible, (The relaxed parts are not to be done loosely, and the tight parts not stiff.) Keep the movement even and smooth and do the set at an even tempo.

Later, when practicing Qigong, the Qi will be felt. Once you feel Qi, only notice it, do not try to direct the flow of Qi to a certain place in the body. Qi sensations may be in various parts of the body, still keep your thoughts on the following movements or on the moment.

If you feel a cold coming on, do the set three times in succession and you will feel better.

It is important to pay attention to where directing the gaze in each movement. Sometimes the gaze looks into the distance and sometimes the gaze is being directed to the hands or at the sky or ground. Each movement will give more detail direction of gaze. This helps to concentrate the Qi in the body.

During the entire set, keep the lips together, the back teeth touching lightly, and gently placing the tip of the tongue on top of the mouth just behind the front teeth. This connects the Ren and Du Channels and permits Qi to flow up the back and down the front of the body, which enhances the connection of the *xiao zhou tian*.

Dayan Qigong
Practice Advice from Master Liu

If one wishes to attain mastery in Dayan Qigong, one must make it a habit to practice it every day. Before practicing, relax the whole body, calm and clear the mind of any distractions. Do not attach your mind to the external surrounding and situations. Focus on every movement and position of your hands, feet, and body. Be attentive to the particulars of each movements, e.g., the placement of the feet and where the weight should be placed. For beginners, practice slowly; do the basic warm-up exercises and then proceed to practice the first 64 movements. If time permits, repeat the set a few more times, especially those who have not learned the entire set. Again, pay attention to the weight and position of your feet and coordinate them in accordance with the principles of yin and yang, empty and full. All in all, it should take about 20 minutes for the first repetition. On the second repetition, the set may be done at regular speed, taking about 10 minutes. On the third repetition, one may execute it even faster but still maintaining a smooth tempo, like "floating clouds and running river"—the movements are natural and lively. Practice well and benefits will gradually arise.

After completing the set, rise slowly and extend the arms and hands to the side of the body to form a large ball of qi and raise it towards the head, then down pass the face and body—essentially providing qi to the upper, middle, and lower *Dantians*. Finally, lower the hands to the side of the body and briefly contemplate the *Hui Yin* point. Remain still for two minutes to let the qi circulate throughout the body.

Never practice Qigong in a windy, rainy, snowy, or foggy environment. Choose a quiet setting near trees and flowers where the air quality is clean and fresh.

When practicing alone, one may do the movements slowly. Verify the accuracy of the movements, the positions of hands and feet, and weight. When giving qi to the acupuncture points, be clear about the correct point location. To heal and nourish a certain area of the body or illness, one may send qi to it more often. Using this approach, the set may take as long as 45 minutes to complete.

Meditation practice complements the active movements of the qigong set. When movement and stillness are practiced accordingly, one is truly practicing Dayan Qigong in its entirety. Dayan Qigong has many forms of stillness practices. Through regular practice, the breath will become longer, deeper, and subtle. Avoid short and coarse breathing and choose a convenient time to meditate. Start with ten minutes and work towards two hours of continuous meditation. Before getting up from meditation, massage or gently pat any areas of discomfort. Dayan Qigong's standing meditation is also a useful and healthy practice. The stance can be high, medium, or low. Maintain the pose for a short time in the beginning and gradually increase the duration over time. This pose is useful for self-examination and uncovering potential health conditions. Upon closing, massage and gently pat the body. At a higher stage of qigong practice, the meridians will be opened and filled with healing qi. Likewise, end your standing practice with an "internal scan" of your body. All in all, movements refine and regulate the qi; stillness nourishes the qi. Practice together will enhance the efficacy of Dayan Qigong.

Dayan Qigong
Practice Advice from Master Liu

Qigong practice requires concentration, perseverance, humility, and a compassionate heart.

Concentration – Relax the body and quiet the mind, clearing it of any discursive thoughts. Be mindful of the present moment. Maintain mental equanimity regardless of how frenetic one's life may be. Without concentration, everything will be met with difficulty.

Perseverance – Perseverance is the basis of success. A scientific experiment requires ten to twenty years of continuous research before achieving success. If an enterprise is abandoned before it could flourish and prosper, not only is profit forfeited, but all past effort would be wasted. Even the simplest form of exercise requires more than three months, how much the more a practice as refined and subtle as qigong?

Humility – It is said, "Humility brings benefit, arrogance invites calamity." Be receptive toward learning and one would make progress. Have a sincere and joyful heart towards one's teachers and colleagues, as conceit would lead to loss of trust. Of all the hexagrams in the I-Ching, only hexagram #15 (*Qian*-Humility) has all positive attributes.

Compassion – Manifest and embody a compassionate and empathetic heart towards all living beings—humans, animals, and plants. As Lao Zi said, "The highest virtue is compassion towards all living beings." A truly compassionate person radiates a peaceful and beautiful smile. Practicing Dayan Qigong, one gains health and achieves wonders of the body and spirit.

Dayan Qigong originated from the Kunlun Mountains. It was created by a Buddhist monk named Dao An 1,700 years ago, during the Eastern Jin dynasty. It has been passed down in secret for 27 generations until Grandmaster Yang Mei Jun taught it to the public. We are very fortunate to have received the complete 64 movements of the first and second set from her. The lineage verse of Dayan Qigong is *"Dao De De Dao Zheng Dao Xing."* To reach the highest mastery of qigong, nurturing one's virtue is absolutely necessary. One must also harmonize water and fire in the body, through *Dantian* practice. Focus on the lower *Dantian*, 1.5 inches behind the navel. After some time, one will naturally feel a warm sensation behind the navel. To facilitate the rising of water, quiet the mind and place the tongue gently behind the palate, with the mouth closed. Eventually, the saliva will be infused with sweetness; and when it fills the mouth, swallow it slowly, with the mind following it to the lower *Dantian*. There will be a warm and moist sensation in the lower *Dantian*. This is the cultivation of one's energy source, as the navel is where an infant connects with her mother prior to birth. It is also the point at which the body's 12 meridians connect with the five organs and six viscera. If qi could be gathered in the lower *Dantian*, the entire body would be nourished and one is bestowed longevity and happiness.

Lao Zi said, "If people are pure and tranquil, heaven and earth return to the primordial." Guan Zi said, "The art of nourishing life can truly benefit a person." Maintain a mind free of worries, sorrow, joy and anger; keep it level and equal. Then and there, one obtains the

Dayan Qigong
Practice Advice from Master Liu

Way. If the mind is agitated, it disappears. Thus, the spiritual qi resides in the heart/mind; when the mind is still, the Way manifests; when the heart is stirred, the Way disappears.

The pillar of Grandmaster Yang's teaching is, "*Dao De, De Dao, Zheng Dao Xin*. When virtue is the path, the proper Way will flourish." If one wishes to attain optimal result from practicing Dayan Qigong, then one must cultivate one's virtue (*De*). Also, how does one retain beneficial energy and live a long life? First, one must achieve balance of Water (yin) and Fire (yang). In the Five Element Theory, the heart (or mind) regulates the fire element. Fire's nature is to ignite and ascend. The heart's role is to ruminate and cogitate, which often leads to anxiety and worries, or afflictions. If the mind is unrestrained, then just like fire, one's energy is exhausted, leading to rapid aging and early death when one's qi is completely consumed. Furthermore, the kidneys regulate the Water element. Water's nature is to descend. And when Fire ascends and Water descends, there is separation of Yang and Yin, Fire and Water, leading to rapid aging and early death. Therefore, to maintain a long and healthy life, Fire and Water must unite in a balanced way. Fire must descend and Water must ascend, as in boiling a pot of water. Practicing qigong and meditation can help achieve the harmony of Fire and Water.

Five Elements 五行

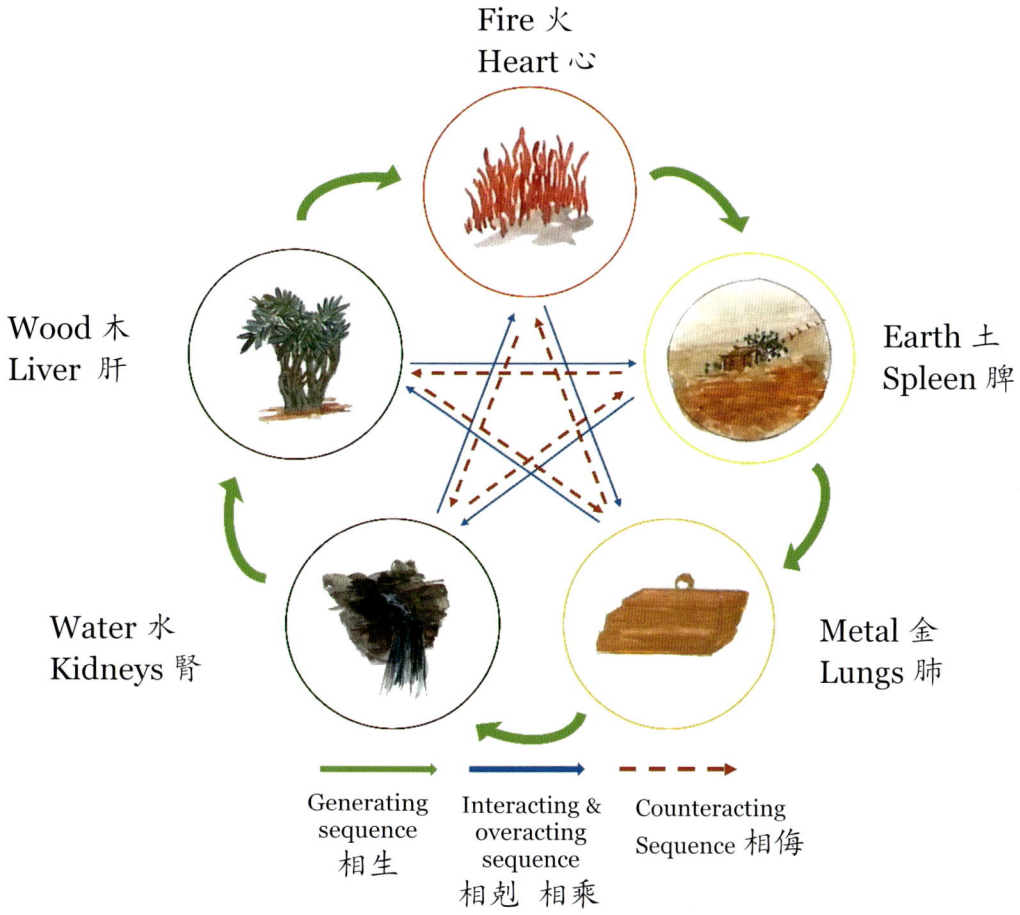

Dayan Qigong
Meridians and Massage Points Explained

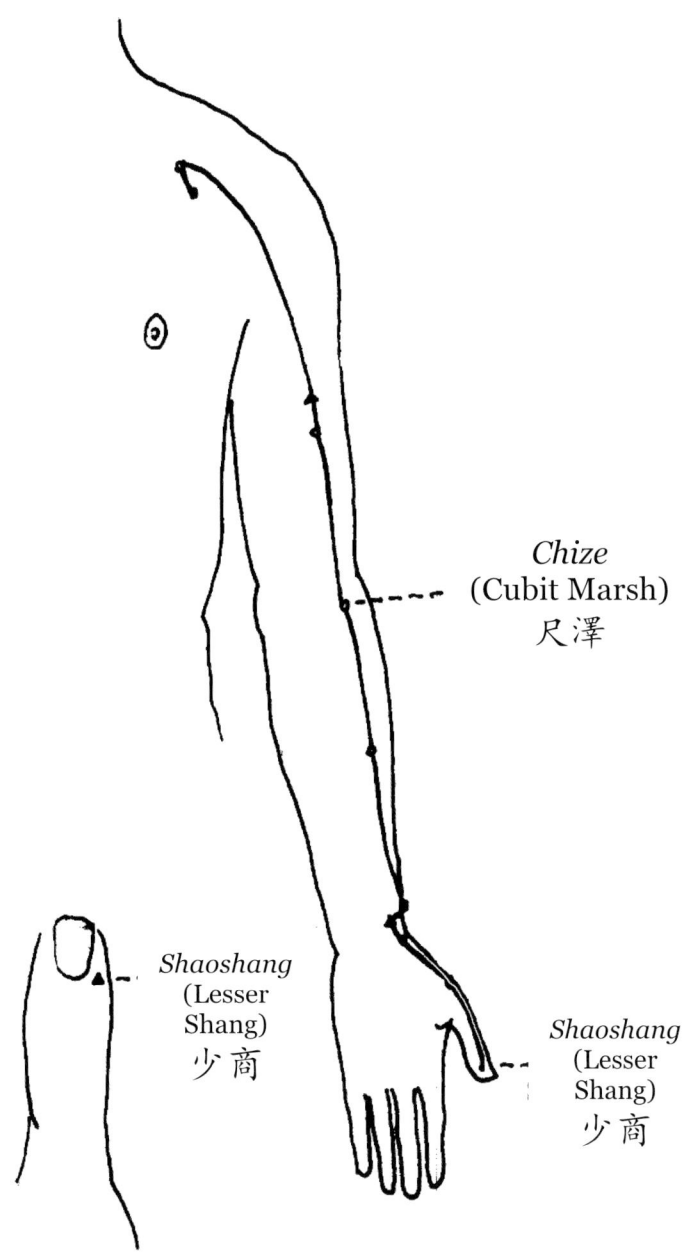

The Lung meridian goes from the chest to the hand.

Chize (LU 5) (Cubit Marsh) located on the cubital crease, in the depression of the radial side of the tendon. This point is located with the elbow slightly flexed.

Lung Meridian

手太陰肺經

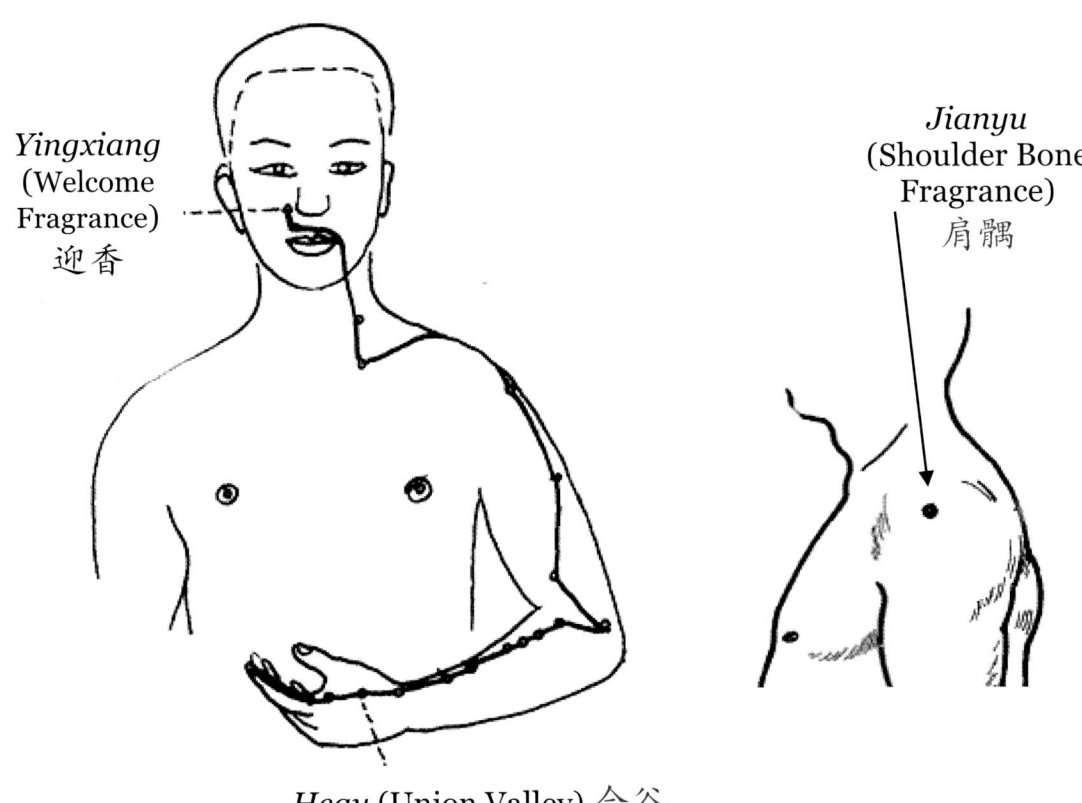

Yingxiang (Welcome Fragrance) 迎香

Jianyu (Shoulder Bone Fragrance) 肩髃

Hegu (Union Valley) 合谷

Large Intestine Meridian

手陽明大腸經

The Large Intestine meridian goes from the hand to the head.

Hegu (LI 4) (Union Valley) located on the dorsum of the hand between the 1st and 2nd metacarpal bones, in the middle of the 2nd metacarpal bone on the radial side.

Yingxiang (LI 20) (Welcome Fragrance) located in the nasolabial groove at level of the midpoint of the lateral border of ala nasi.

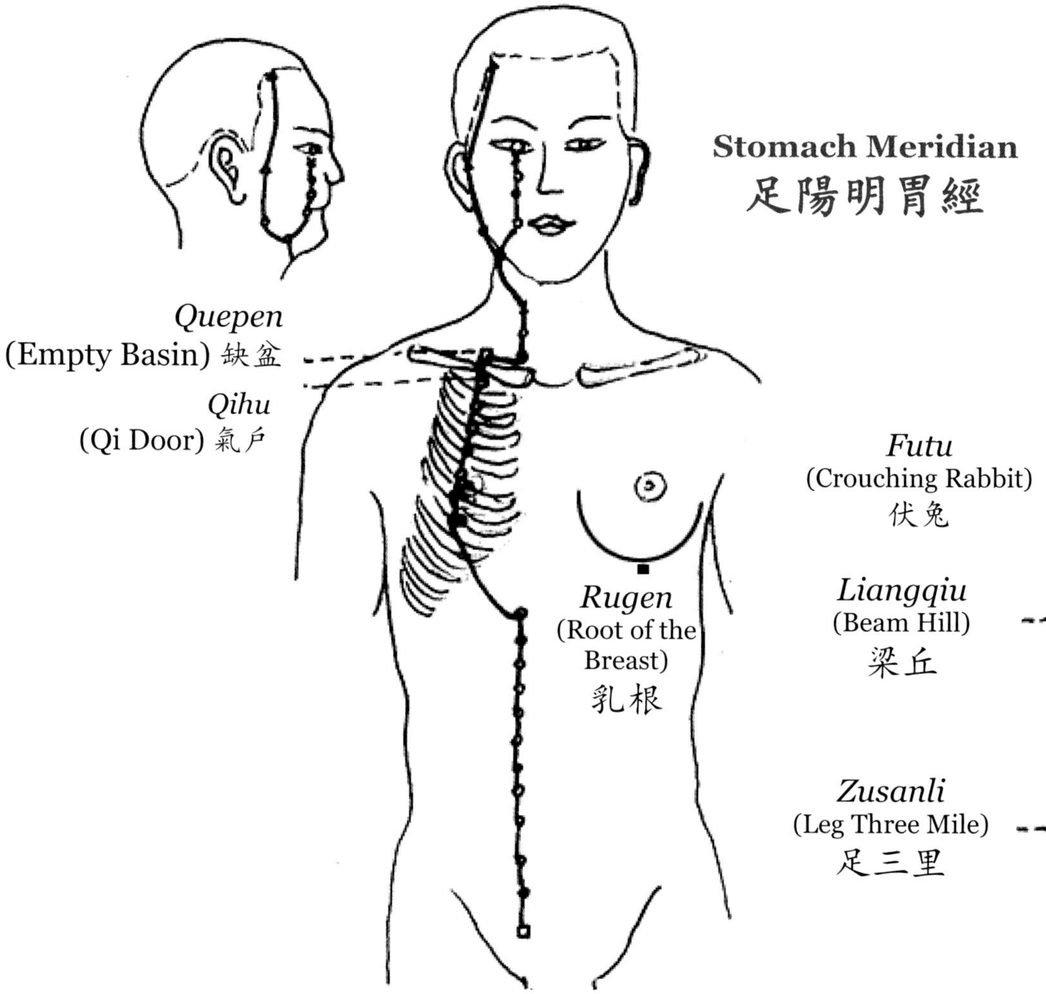

Dayan Qigong
Meridians and Massage Points Explained

Stomach Meridian
足陽明胃經

Quepen (Empty Basin) 缺盆

Qihu (Qi Door) 氣戶

Rugen (Root of the Breast) 乳根

Futu (Crouching Rabbit) 伏兔

Liangqiu (Beam Hill) 梁丘

Zusanli (Leg Three Mile) 足三里

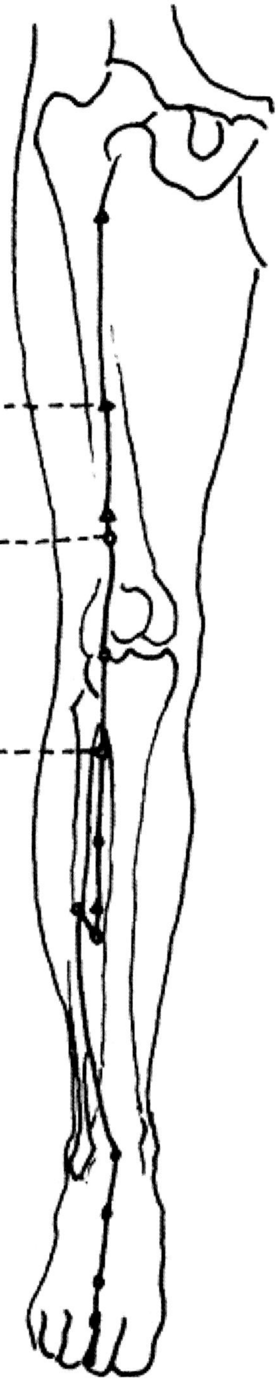

The Stomach meridian goes from the head to the foot.

Quepen (ST 12) (Empty Basin) located in the midpoint of the supraclavicular fossa, 4 cun (see page 154) lateral to the anterior midline.

Qihu (ST 13) (Qi Door) located at the lower border of the middle of the clavicle, 4 cun lateral to the anterior midline.

Liangqiu (ST 34) (Beam Hill) located when the knee is flexed, the point is 2 cun above the lateral upper border of the patella.

Zusanli (ST 36) (Leg 3 Miles) located 3 cun below the lower tip of the patella, and one finger-breath from the anterior border of the tibia.

Spleen Meridian
足太陰脾經

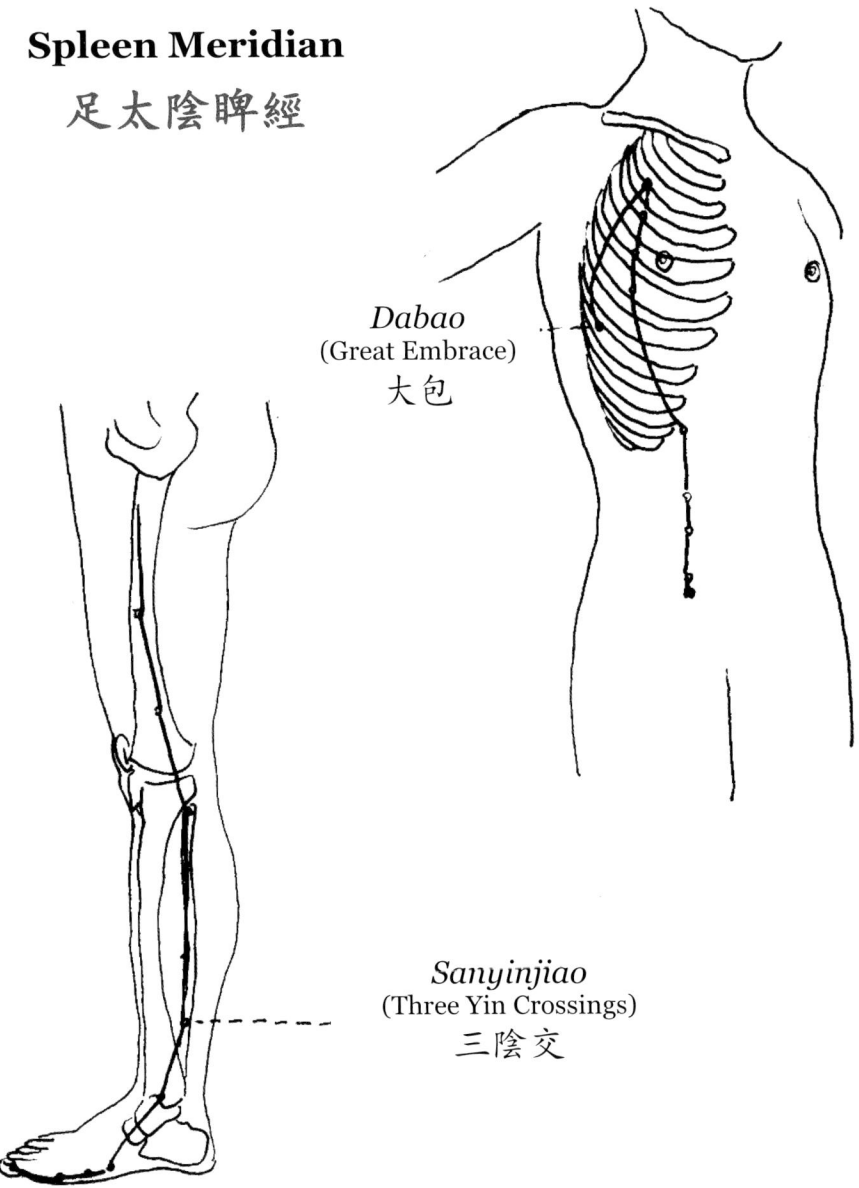

The Spleen meridian goes from the foot through the abdomen to the chest. *Sanyinjiao* (SP 6) (Three Yin Crossing) is located 3 cun directly above the tip of the medial malleolus, posterior to the medial border of the tibia. *Dabao* (SP 21) (Great Embracement) located on the lateral side of the chest and on the middle axillary line, in the 6th intercostal space.

Dayan Qigong
Meridians and Massage Points Explained

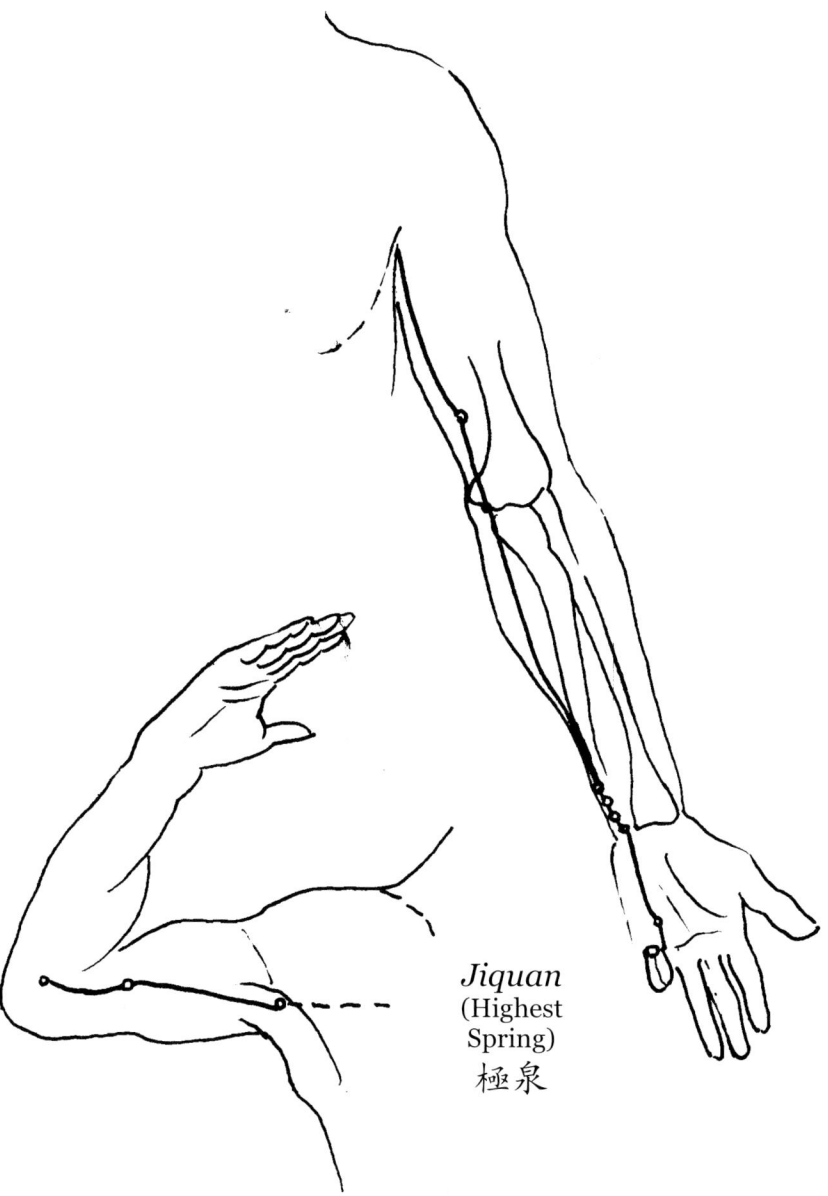

The Heart meridian goes from the chest to the hand.

Jiquan (HT 1) (Highest Spring) located when the upper arm is abducted, the point is in the center of the axilla, on the medial side of the axillary artery.

Jiquan
(Highest Spring)
極泉

Heart Meridian
手少陰心經

Dayan Qigong
Meridians and Massage Points Explained

The Small Intestine meridian goes from the hand to the ear.

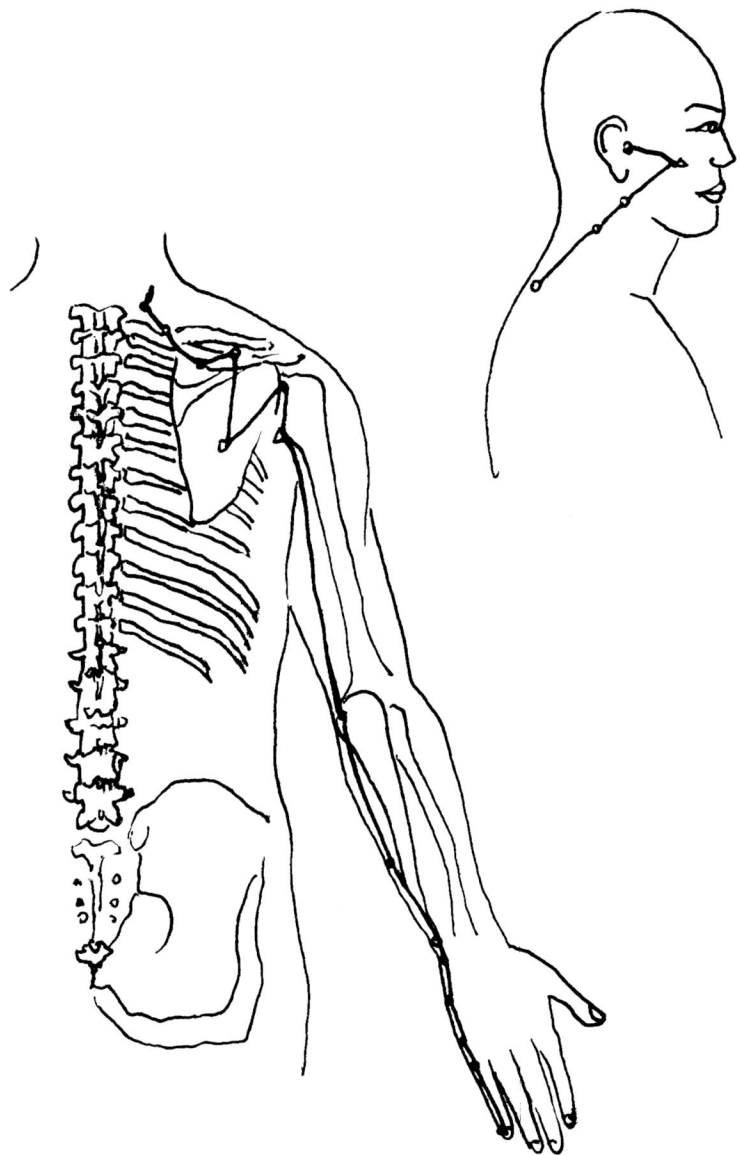

Small Intestine Meridian
手太陽小腸經

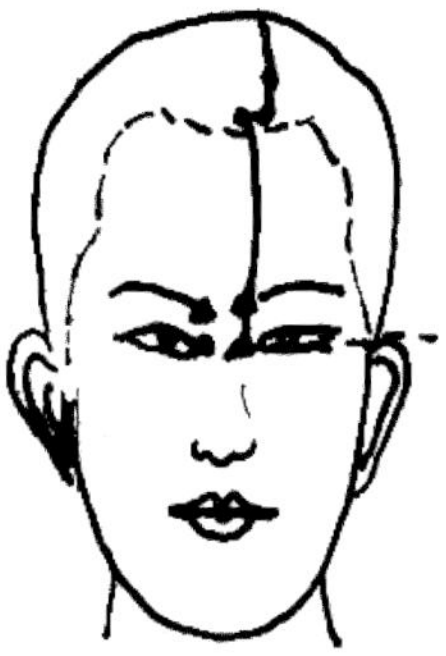

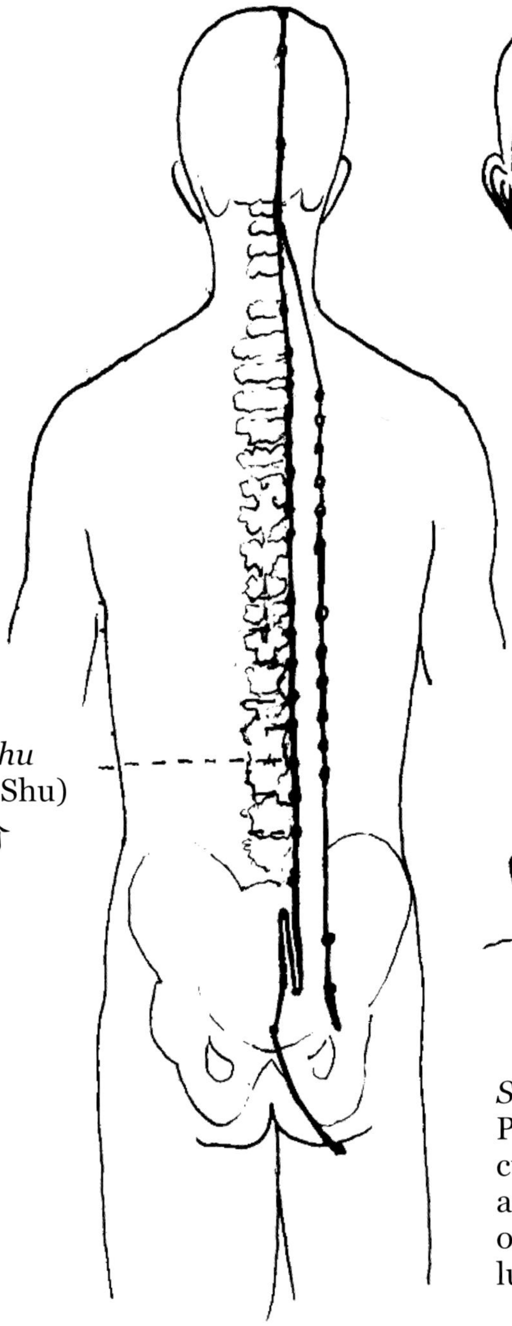

Dayan Qigong
Meridians and Massage Points Explained

Jingming
(Bright Eye)
晴明

The Urinary Bladder meridian goes from the head to the foot.

Jingming (UB 1) (Bright Eyes) located in the depression slightly above the inner canthus.

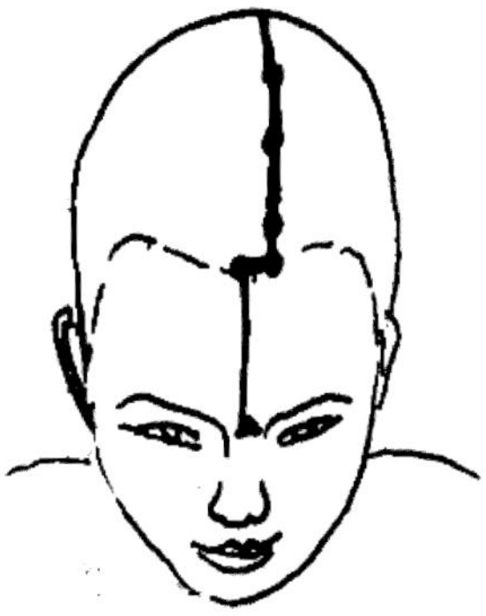

Shenshu
(Kidney Shu)
腎俞

Shenshu (UB 23) (The back Shu Point of the Kidney) located 1.5 cun lateral to *Mingmen* (GV 4), at the level of the lower border of the spinous process of the 2nd lumbar vertebrae.

Urinary Bladder Meridian
足太陽膀胱經

Dayan Qigong
Meridians and Massage Points Explained

Urinary Bladder continues from pelvis down to foot

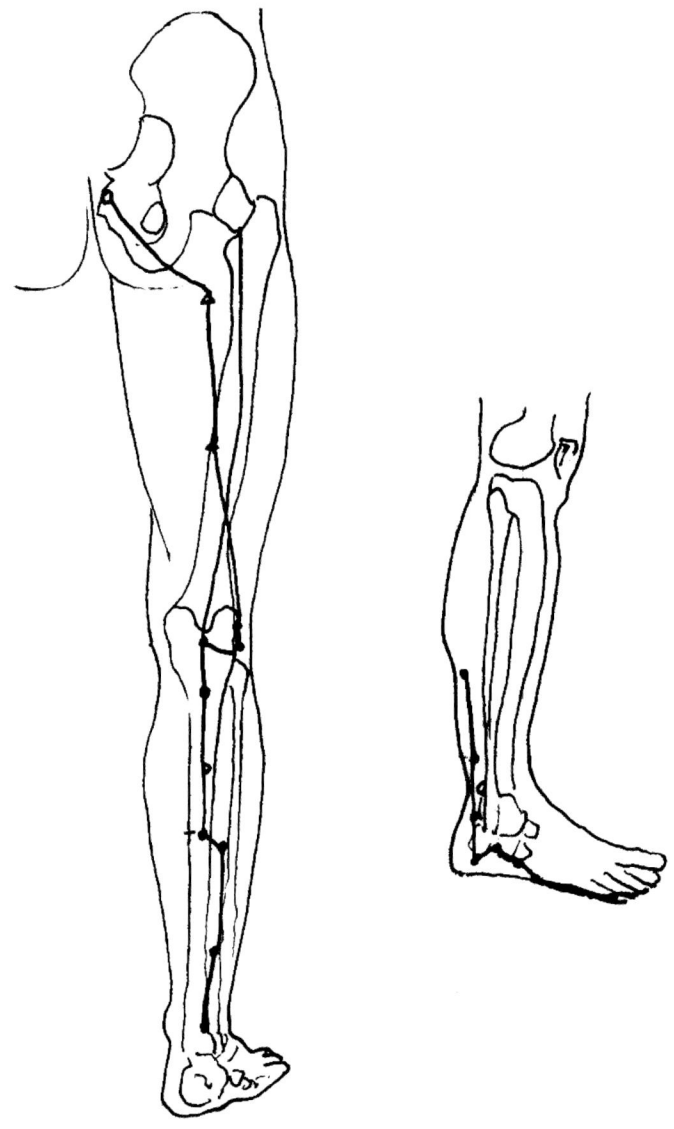

Urinary Bladder Meridian
足太陽膀胱經

Dayan Qigong
Meridians and Massage Points Explained

The Kidney meridian goes from the foot to the abdomen (chest).

Qihai
(Sea of Qi)
氣海

Yongquan
(Gushing Spring)
涌泉

Yongquan (KI 1) (Great Spring) located on the sole, in the depression on a line connecting to the 2nd and 3rd toes

Kidney Meridian
足少陰腎經

Dayan Qigong
Meridians and Massage Points Explained

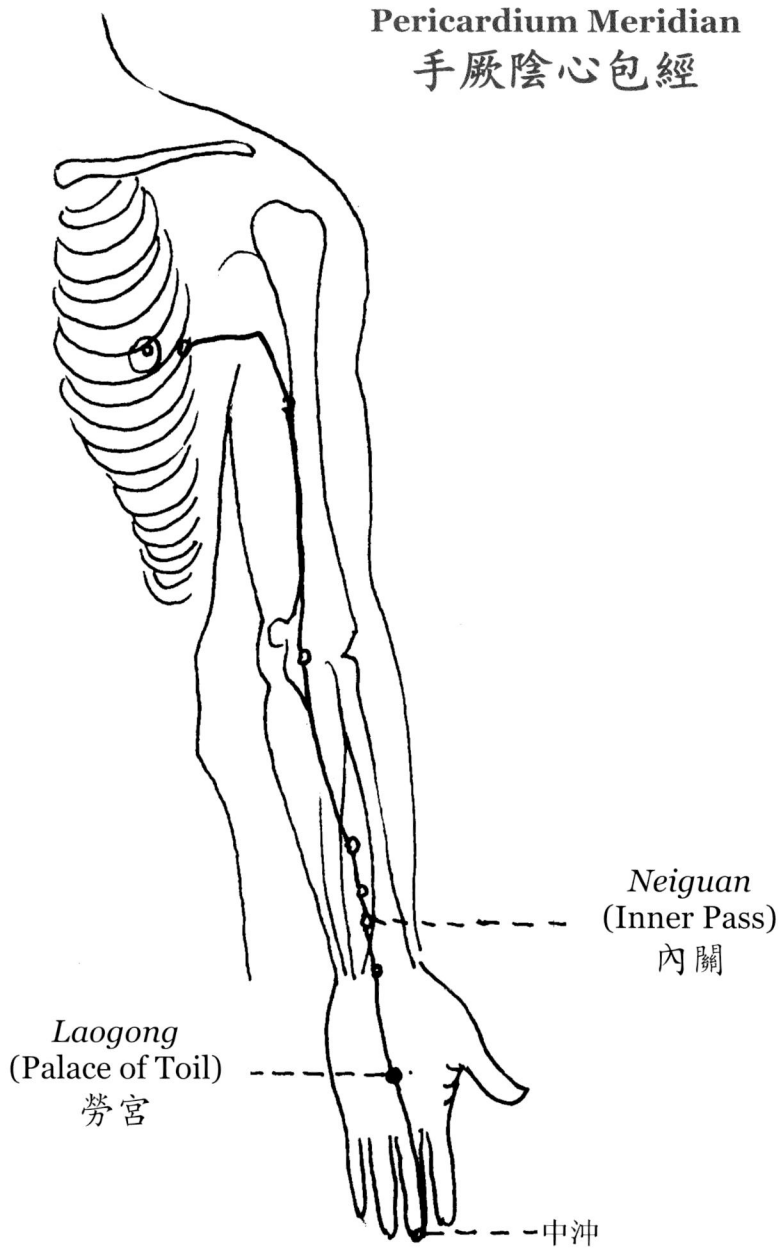

The Pericardium meridian goes from the chest to the hand.

Neiguan (PC 6) (Inner Pass) located 2 cun above the transverse crease of the wrist, between the tendons.

Laogong (PC 8) (Palace of Toil) located at the center of the palm between the 3rd and 4th metacarpal bones, touching the tip of the middle finger when a fist is made.

Dayan Qigong
Meridians and Massage Points Explained

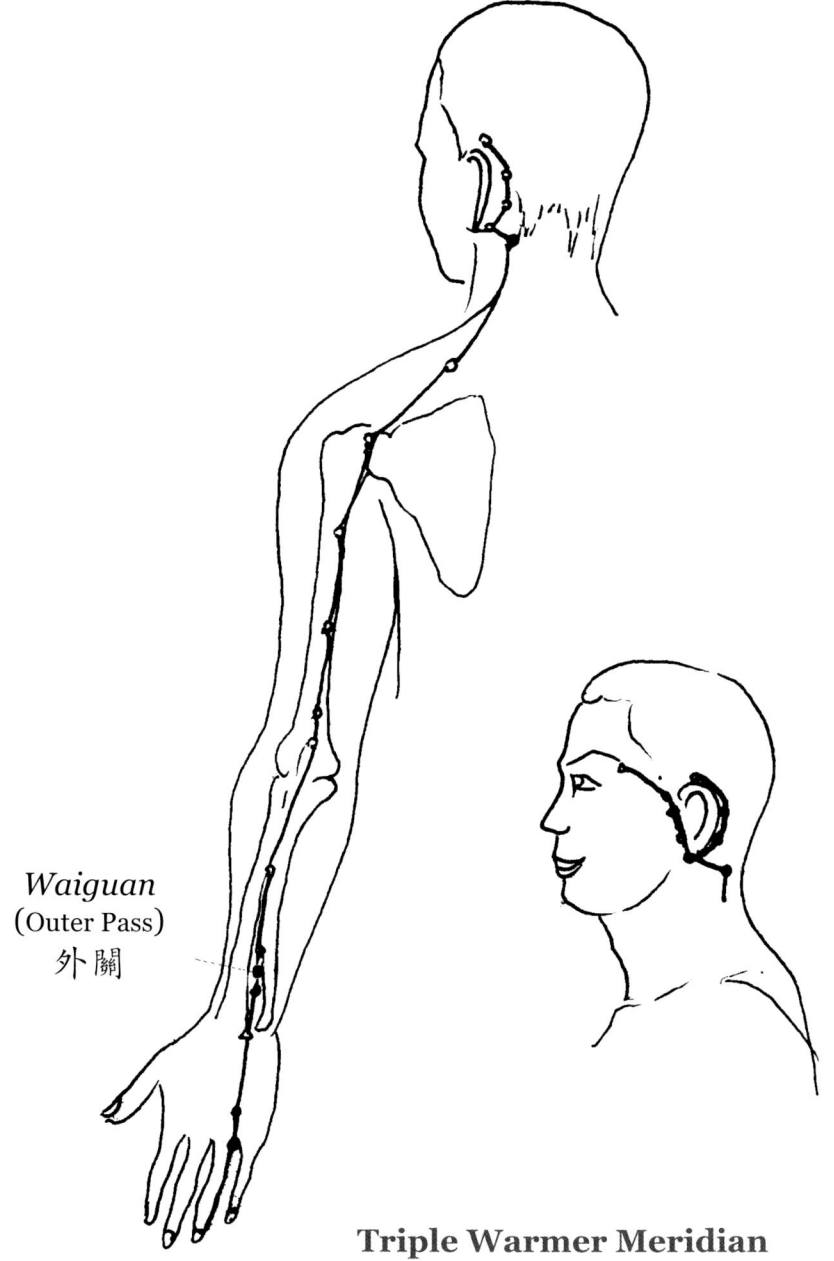

Waiguan
(Outer Pass)
外關

Triple Warmer Meridian
手少陽三焦經

The Triple Warmer meridian goes from the back of the hand, up the back of the arm, back of the shoulder, up the neck, behind the ear, to the head.

Waiguan (TW 5) (Outer Pass) located 2 cun proximal to the dorsal crease of the wrist, between the radius and ulna.

Dayan Qigong
Meridians and Massage Points Explained

The Gallbladder meridian goes from the head to the foot.

Huantiao (GB 30) (Jumping Round) located at the junction of the lateral 1/3 and medial 2/3 of the distance between the prominence of the greater trochanter and the hiatus of the sacrum.

Huantiao
(Jumping Round)
環跳

Huantiao
(Jumping Round)
環跳

Gallbladder Meridian
足少陽膽經

Dayan Qigong
Meridians and Massage Points Explained

The Liver meridian goes from the foot to the abdomen (chest).

Sanyinjiao (SP 6) (Three Yin Crossing) located 3 cun directly above the tip of the medial malleolus, posterior to the medial border of the tibia.

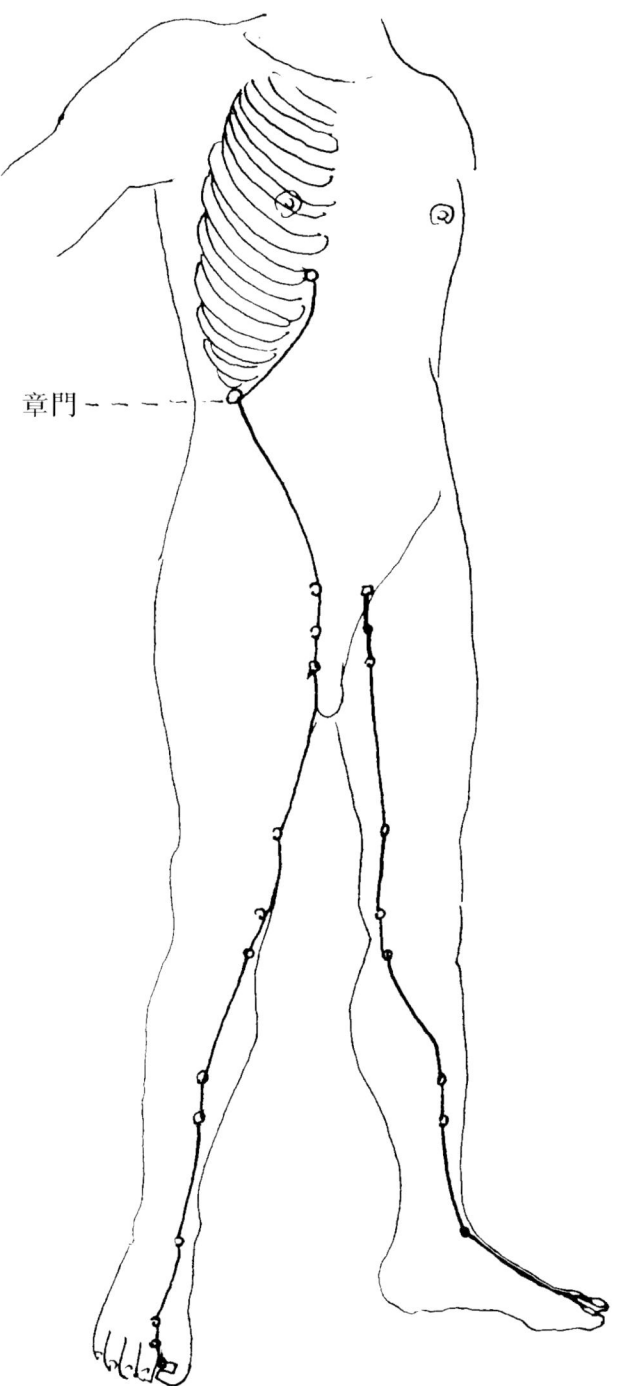

章門

Liver Meridian
足厥陰肝經

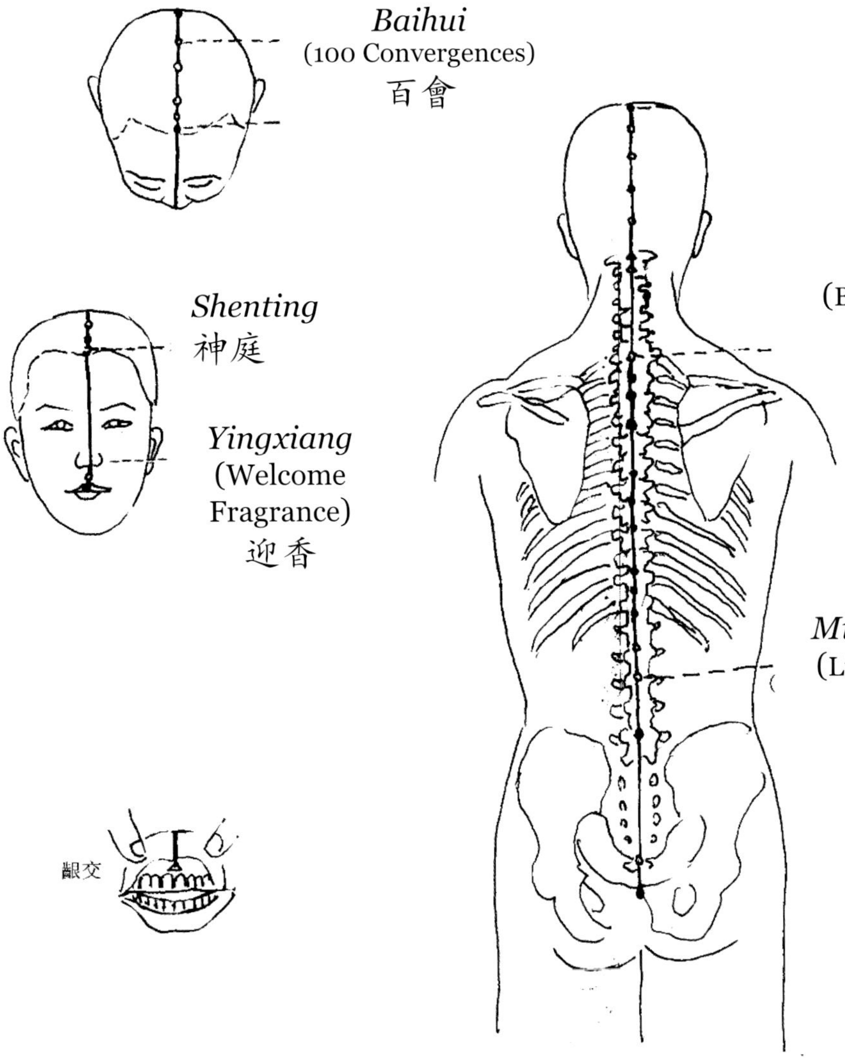

Dayan Qigong
Meridians and Massage Points Explained

Du Meridian
督脈

The Du or Governor Vessel goes along the back midline.

Baihui (GV 20) (100 Convergences) located on the Du or Governor Vessel on the midline of the head, 5 cun directly above the midpoint of the anterior hairline, and on the midpoint of the line connecting the apexes of both ears.

Mingmen (GV 4) (Life Gate) located on the Du or Governor Vessel meridian below the spinous process of the second lumbar vertebrae.

Dayan Qigong
Meridians and Massage Points Explained

Ren Meridian
任脈

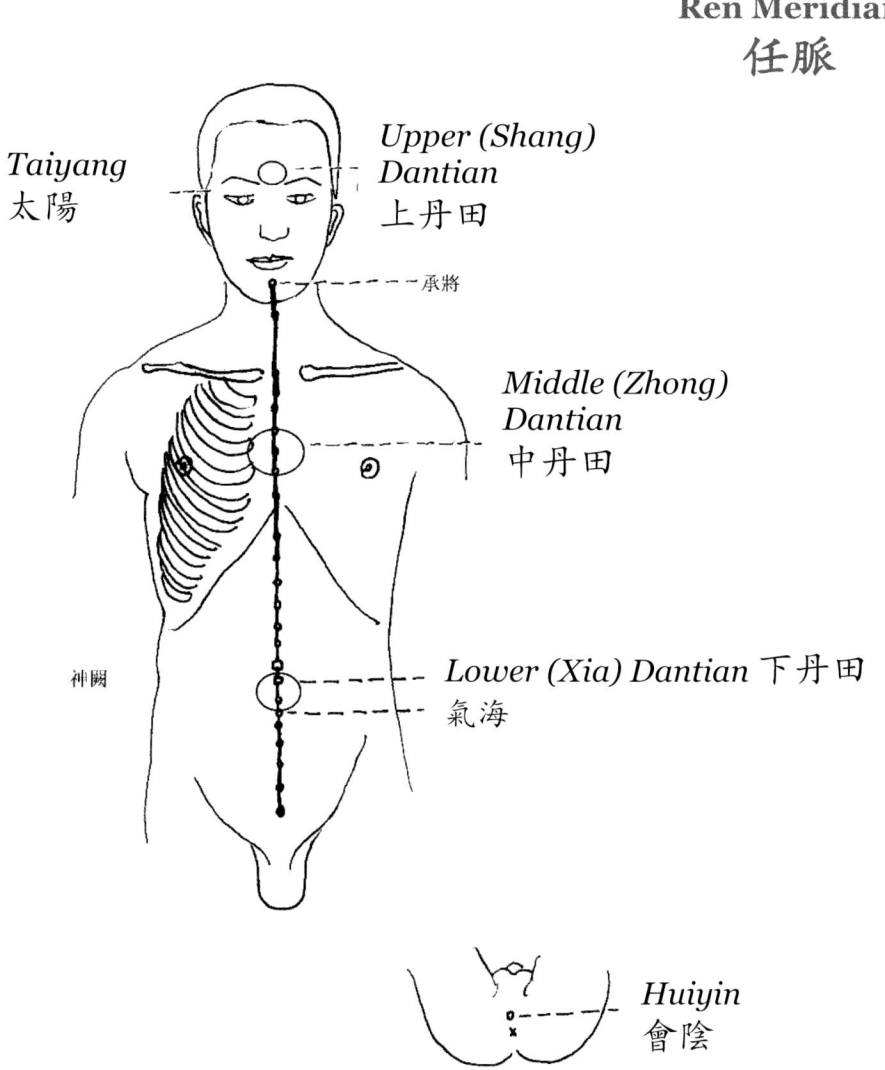

The Ren or Conception Vessel goes along the front midline.

Shang *Dantian* (Upper)
Zhong *Dantian* (Middle)
Tanzhong (CV 17) located on the Ren or Conception Vessel on the anterior midline, at the level with the fourth intercostal space, midway between the nipples.
Xia *Dantian* (Lower)

Dayan Qigong
Meridians and Massage Points Explained

All Meridians and Massage points

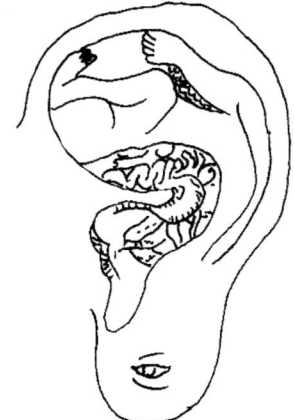

Ear resembles inverted fetus
耳部正如胚胎倒影

Lung (肺)

Large Intestine (大腸)

Heart (心)

Small Intestine (小腸)

Triple Warmer (三焦)

Pericardium (心包)

Bladder (膀胱)

Liver (肝)

Spleen (脾)

Gallbladder (膽)

Stomach (胃)

Insomnia (*shimian* 失眠)

Yongquan (涌泉)

172

Dayan Qigong
Meridians and Massage Points Explained

Measurement of the Body's Inch

When the middle finger is flexed, the distance between the two medial ends of the creases of the interphalangeal joints equals one cun, which is one body inch.

Between these 2 joints is equal to one body inch or one cun.

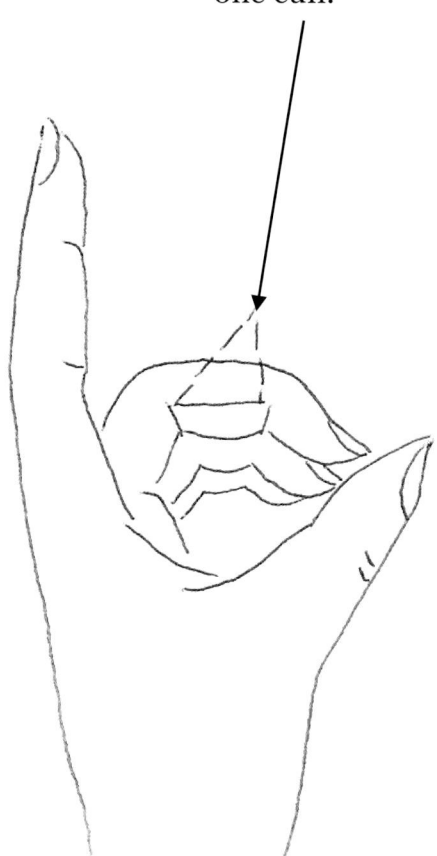

Dayan Qigong
Chinese Tea Ceremony

Chinese tea has a tradition of over 4,000 years. According to legends, Shen Nong, also known as the father of Chinese medicine, ingested 72 different kinds of poisons for his medical research. Using all kinds of herbs, he was unable to rid his body of the poisons. Finally, he stumbled upon tea leaves which he used successfully to eradicate the poisons from his system.

In China, the Confucius, Tao, and Buddhist schools all rely on tea for their physical and spiritual development. The art of drinking tea is grounded in profound philosophy and is considered a cultural treasure of China. Tea is best appreciated in a natural, quiet, and clean environment. Care should be taken to ensure that all the tea implements are made of natural material such as clay, bamboo, wood, and stone, nonmetal or plastic.

Tea may be enjoyed in five ways: using the eyes to appreciate the color, the nose to sense the fragrance, the mouth to taste the flavor, the ears to listen to the opening tea leaves and flowing water (requires quiet and stillness), and the heart to contemplate and evoke the spiritual benefits. This is truly life's finest pleasure.

Drinking tea requires careful selection of water, tea, and pot.

The best water is clear, natural, or purified filtered water. Water should also be cold, light, low in minerals, and a little natural sweet tasting.

Tea
There are many types of tea: green, red, oolong, white, black, yellow, and fruit tea.

Green tea includes Tie Guan Yin, Bao Zhong, Qing Cha, light oolong, Long Jing, Gao Shan, and Pi Luo Quan. Each tea is processed in a unique way and has many grades of quality.

Pots
Many types of pots may be used for tea: i-xing ceramic, iron, and porcelain.

For green tea, i-xing pots are ideal. I-xing clay is highly malleable, strong, nonstick to the hands, and when baked, is strong and not subjected to expansion and contraction, thus retaining the pot's original shape and design. I-xing clay has excellent thermal retention, making it relatively safe to handle with bare hands. Continuous use and polishing with the hands will add luster to the i-xing pots. I-xing pots also have 18 different minerals that can benefit the body.

When selecting a pot, pay attention to the pot's material, design, and artistry. Good clay will have a high ringing, metallic sound. A well-design pot has the following characteristics:
- a clay filter inside with a minimum of seven holes
- the lid fits securely on the pot
- the handle should be big enough for your fingers

- the spout should line up with the handle
- the spout should pour water forcefully and straight, without any dribbling

Pots are also appreciated for their artistic qualities. Many pots have fine carvings and calligraphy. Often times, pots are collected by connoisseurs and may be more valuable than gold or jade.

When drinking tea, small cups are preferred. The cups should be made with porcelain on the inside so that the color of the tea may be seen, and ceramic on the outside to match with the pot. Glass is also acceptable.

18 Steps to Making Tea

1. Start boiling the water. Prepare all the implementations of tea: pots, utensils, clips, tray, and bowls. High quality green tea should be close by. A vase of flower on the tea table enhances the experience.
2. Place the teapot in a bowl and pour boiling water to overfill the tea pot. This warms and cleans the pot.
3. Use the water from the pot to warm and clean the cups.
4. Pour remaining water to an empty bowl and discard water.
5. Use a bamboo tea scoop to extract the appropriate amount of tea from the tea container. The amount varies depending on your personal taste or diet. For example, more tea should be used after eating a lot of greasy food or meat; vegetarians may use a lighter amount. Also, in the morning, it is best to use a lighter amount.
6. Let the boiling water cool to about 90 degree Celsius. Then pour water into the tea pot in a circular pattern. Tea connoisseurs like to pour water from a foot above the pot. Pour the water to completely fill up the pot.
7. Use the tea stick to sweep laterally the excess foam from tea pot.
8. Cover the pot with the lid.
9. Immediately drain the pot into an empty tea bowl. This cleans the tea and the excess tea water; when cooled, the water can be used on the plants.
10. Repeat steps 6 to 8
11. Pour boiling water over the covered pot and the outside of the pot.
12. Discard the water in cups from step 3 to tea bowl.
13. Keep tea in pot for 30 – 60 seconds.
14. Pour tea in cup in circular, uniform, and even pattern.
15. If serving to more than one cup, for example 3 cups, follow this pattern: pour 25% in cup 1, 25% in cup 2, and 25% in cup 3; pour 25% more to cup 3, 25% more in cup 2, and 25% more in cup 1; pour 25% more in cup 1, 25% more in cup 2, and 25% more in cup 3. Repeat this pattern until all cups are full. This pattern ensures that the flavor of the tea is consistent in all cups.
16. Do not let water sit in the pot between drinks. This will make the tea too strong and dissipates the flavor.
17. If drinking Spring or young leaf green tea, keep the lid half open between drinks to maintain freshness.

18. Drink while tea is hot and when you have 1/3 cup left, repeat step 11. But this time, let the tea steep about 10 seconds longer.

It is recommended that one drinks two cups of green tea per day.

Benefits of green tea
- regulate body's metabolism
- increases the immune and physiological systems of body
- fights cancer
- slows aging process and reduces wrinkles
- high in vitamin C , vitamin E, and anti-oxidant compounds

Other benefits of tea
- put tea leaves in your mouth to quench thirst and increase concentration if no boiling water is available
- use wet tea leaves to relieve pimples, inflamed tissues, or cold sores and other infections
- use cotton swab of strong tea to relieve athlete's foot
- strong tea may help in stopping external, superficial bleeding
- hot tea steam may be used to treat tired, red, and swollen eyes
- rinse mouth with tea to strengthen teeth, reduce oral infections, and fight bad breath
- tea is good for bathing and washing hair
- rinsed tea water can be used to water plants
- place dried tea leaves at the bottom of a flower pot and then add soil and plant; this improves circulation in the pot.
- use dried tea leaves as fillings for a sleeping pillow to brighten eyesight and benefit neurological functions
- add tea liquid or powder to make porridge, cookies, noodles, ice cream, etc.

Tea plantations in China and Taiwan

Dayan Qigong
Chinese Tea Ceremony

Master Hui Liu and Master Chiang tea demonstration

Porcelain tea set with tea leaves in dishes

Dayan Qigong
Chinese Tea Ceremony

Chinese special clay tea set

Decorative tea set

Dayan Qigong
Chinese Tea Ceremony

Different shape tea set

Tea Set

Dayan Qigong
Chinese Tea Ceremony

People all over the world are becoming aware that eating good food can affect and improve your health. For centuries, the Chinese have observed that herbs, and certain foods have special specific, if subtle, health-enhancing capacities and properties. They are staples in the traditional Chinese diet, and they are becoming more widely known and used in Western cooking.

Sesame Seeds

Sesame seeds, raw or roasted, eaten whole, ground or as an oil (but only if the oil is the very highest quality) can benefit certain organs and enrich and revitalize blood and Qi. A daily complement of sesame in your diet will tone the spleen, keep the liver and kidneys strong, and help to keep the heart healthy. It also helps to lubricate the intestines, build muscles, tendons, and bones, and keep the bone marrow strong. Two tablespoons of sesame seeds eaten each day are recommended for maximum benefit. It is richer in iron than any other single food.

100 grams of sesame provides:

21.9 gm protein
61.7 gm unsaturated fat
564 mg calcium
338 mg phosphorous
59 mg iron

Ways to Use Sesame Seeds:

1. Grind to a paste and add about 1 tsp. dry rice wine or sweet wine and honey or brown sugar to taste.
2. Grind equal amounts of rice and sesame. Add water and boil, turn to lower heat until the mixture reaches the consistency of gruel.

Lau Fu Zi, a Jin Dynasty poet, wrote about the sesame seed in his book on health and longevity. His recipe is as follows:

> Take 3 liters of sesame seeds;
> Steam 9 times and dry 9 times in the Sun;
> Stir fry until they are powdery;
> Add honey;
> Roll sesame into size of a marble ball;
> Eat sesame and drink warm rice wine;
> Do this three times a day for 100 days to cure persistent illnesses;
> In one year your face will look glowing and you will feel less hungry;
> In two years gray hair will return to its natural color;
> In three years you will grow new teeth;
> In four years you will be impervious to fire and flood;

In five years you will be as swift and fleet of foot as a horse;
Do this for more than five years and you will achieve immortality.

Soybeans

The soybean is called "king of the bean family". Three thousand years ago Chinese doctors found that soybeans can benefit the kidneys, circulate water and Qi, relieve fever, improve blood circulation, and detoxify poisons. Eaten consistently over a long period, soybeans can help to build muscles, improve the complexion, increase production of bone marrow, and increase energy.

Soybeans contain approximately 40% protein, or approximately the same amount of protein that is found in animal products. It also contains the complete complement of essential amino acids that meat has. Soybeans have been called "plant meat" or "the green cow". They also contain 18-20% fat, though it is healthier than animal fat since it contains significantly less cholesterol.

100 grams of soybeans provides:

   367 mg calcium

   571 mg phosphate

   11 mg iron

The calcium in soybeans helps prevent bone softening in children and loss of calcium in the elderly. The body easily absorbs this form of iron.

Nine European hospitals conducted a study of 127 people, giving them soybeans in various forms instead of meat. After 8 weeks, the cholesterol level was found to have decreased by 23% in men and by 25% in women. There are no obvious side effects from eating soybeans.

Soybean products include sprouts and soybean cheese or curd, known as tofu. Soybean sprouts contain ten times more Vitamin B12 than red meat, and a significant amount of vitamin C. Cooked sprouts benefit spleen, stomach and urinary bladder meridians, aid digestion, relieve edema, and strengthen blood. Tofu has about 3 times more protein than whole milk, but only half the calories. It also has 2 times as much calcium and 3 times more iron. Tofu sheets (the dried skim from tofu milk) have 47 times more protein than cheese, one third less fat, 8 times more calcium, 9 times more iron, 43 times more phosphate and only 60% of the calories of cheese. The chemical makeup of soybeans is similar to that of black beans.

Red Dates

One of the "Five Fruits" in ancient China, red dates can increase Qi and calm the mind. The sugar content of dates is higher than that of sugar cane--fresh dates contain 20-36% sugar and preserved dates contain 55-80% sugar. 100 grams of fresh dates contain 380-

600 mg of Vitamin C. It has been called "The living Vitamin C Pill". (Incidentally, this form of Vitamin C is much more usable by the body than a pill.) Lemons are the symbol of high Vitamin P (a term sometimes used to denote the bioflavonoid, related to Vitamin C), but red dates have ten times more. Vitamin P can strengthen blood vessels and is very beneficial to people with high blood pressure and heart diseases. 100 grams of dates also contains 1.2 grams of protein, 0.2 grams of fat, and 0.5 grams of iron.

Chinese medical books mention that red dates can expel stagnant Qi, clear the mind, strengthen Qi in the spleen, benefit Qi in the stomach, increase the function in the 12 meridians, and supplement insufficient Qi. Continuous intake of red dates will make the body light and give long life. Other benefits cited are moistening lungs, stop coughing, and strengthening the heart, liver, stomach, spleen, and kidney. It is very beneficial for spleen problems. Four or five dates should be eaten each day.

Here is an ancient prescription:

Boil 10 dates, 30 grams of whole wheat and 9 grams of licorice together into a soup. It is good for regulating anemia, increasing blood platelets, reducing excessive perspiration during menopause, calming a restless mind and quelling sudden anger.

There is an ancient song describing how dates can help heartaches:

Take one dried plum, 2 dates and 7 almonds and blend well. Men drink with wine, women drink with vinegar, and no heartache ever.

There is a tale about dates:

There was a village, which for centuries had produced dates. It was said that if one should eat a date without a stone one could achieve immortality. One day a woman actually did get a date with no stone, and never again did she have to eat, she got married at 50 years old, and her appearance was that of a teenager.

Recipes using dates for various ailments:

1. Stomachache: Remove pits from dried dates. Roast over low heat until dried and crush to a powder. For every 9 grams of dates add 3 grams of ginger root. Swallow with water. This is for regulating Qi in the stomach.

2. Annoyed, depressed, and/or insomnia: 20 dates and 7 green onions.

3. Anemia: 100 grams of dates, cooked into a thick broth. Eat the dates and drink the liquid, 3 times a day.

4. Cirrhosis and hepatitis: Cook into soup 200 grams dates and 9 grams Ying Chen (a Chinese herb, aka, Artemisia herba). Drink morning and evening. Or, one tael, (one and one third ounce) each of dates, peanuts, and rock sugar. Cook the peanuts first, then add the dates and sugar. Take morning and night for 30 days.

5. Weak Qi and abnormal perspiration: Combine 10 dates, 10 grams of preserved plums, 10 grams of mulberry leaves, and 15 grams of wheat and cook in water, or combine 12 dates, 2 taels, (each tael equals 1 and ½ ounce) black beans, 1 tael Huang Qi (Astragalus Radix) and boil in water. Of either, take two portions once a day.

6. Prolapse of the rectum: Take 120 grams of dates and 1/2 pound aged vinegar. Cook until all the vinegar has evaporated and eat the dates.

Note: Not only is the date nutritious, but the pits, its tree bark, leaves and root are all considered medicinal. They are all beneficial to the stomach, spleen, liver, and blood. Never eat rotten dates. Dates can be eaten fresh, cooked in soup, as filling in sweet buns, or even included in meat stew.

Walnuts

Walnuts are called "long-life fruits" in China for two reasons: the walnut tree lives a very long time, usually a few hundred years, and walnuts are very nutritious, strengthening the kidneys and brain, and contribute to living to an old age. Walnuts contain 40-50% fat, mainly glycerin, 15% protein, and 10% carbohydrates. They also have calcium, iron, phosphorous, carotene, and Vitamin E.

Some known benefits of walnuts are: supplementing Qi and blood, dissolving phlegm, warming the lungs, moistening the intestines, curing coughs, relieving low back and muscle pain, strengthening the teeth, and nourishing the hair. It is also good for urinary problems and prolonged menstruation. For general health, four or five walnuts should be eaten each day.

Doctors in the Tang Dynasty believed that walnuts can keep blood vessels clean and clear of blockages, moisten blood vessels, and make the skin smooth and younger-looking.

Recipes using walnuts for various aliments:

1. Weak lungs and kidneys, prolonged cough and excessive phlegm: 1 or 2 walnuts and 1 or 2 slices of ginger, chewed and swallowed slowly in morning and evening.

2. Impotence and spermatorrhea: Eat 60 grams of raw walnuts a day for a month.

3. Excessive urination: Bake walnuts, and chew and swallow them with warm wine before sleeping.

4. Urinary bladder stones: (a) 4 taels (each tael equals 1 and ½ ounce) each walnuts and sesame oil. Fry the walnuts in the oil until crisp. Grind them with 4 taels of sugar.

   Mix with the sesame oil remaining. Divide it into 6 parts and take 3 times a day for 2 days. Or (b) 120 grams of walnuts and rock sugar. Fry walnuts in sesame oil until crisp. Grind with the rock sugar into a fine powder. Divide into 30 to 60 gram portions and take 3 or 4 times a day with warm water.

5. Weak kidneys and lower back pain: Take 60 grams of walnuts. Chop into small pieces and mix with warm wine and brown sugar.
6. Weak lungs, kidneys, and asthma: 6 grams each of ginseng and walnuts. Boil together in water and drink as a tea.
7. Cough: With low or absent fever, and clear or white sputum: Eat one walnut with ginger. With high fever and yellow sputum: Eat one walnut with sugar.

Garlic

Garlic contains protein, fat, carbohydrates, Vitamin B-complex, Vitamin C, calcium, phosphorous, iron, and other minerals. It has been proven to be very beneficial in the prevention and cure of high cholesterol levels. Experimenters in West Germany gave patients with high cholesterol levels 3 grams of garlic every day and found that their blood cholesterol was lowered substantially. Garlic extract is very effective in killing bacteria, and chewing garlic for five minutes can kill bacteria in the mouth.

Current research shows that the carotene content in garlic can kill cancer cells. Statistics from tumor studies in China show that in areas where garlic is regularly eaten the incidence of cancer is only one-third of that in other areas. Garlic also stimulates digestion.

Garlic has a long history. It was part of a healthy diet for athletes in Ancient Greece. The Romans used it to cure colds, asthma, and measles. The Persians found that garlic stimulated blood circulation, making the hands and feet warm. Indian doctors in the 5th century found that eating garlic often can increase the I.Q. and make the voice loud and clear. In China various medical books indicate that garlic is very good for the body in many ways.

It is best to eat garlic raw, pressed or grounded. Six cloves are best each day for general health. Scallions and onions have similar effects, but less effective.

Carrots

Carrots contain a high amount of beta carotene, which has been found to play a role in the prevention of cancer. One part of beta carotene is converted by the body into two parts of Vitamin A in a form which is easily utilized by the body and does not accumulate to toxicity. Recent research has found that people with less vitamin A in their diet tend to have twice the incidence of cancer than those who eat more foods containing beta carotene and Vitamin A. Other elements found in carrots increase immunity against cancer and seem to indirectly kill cancer cells. Eating carrots, or any fruit or vegetable containing high amounts of beta carotene (yellow and orange fruits and vegetables and leafy vegetables) seems to help prevent lung cancer. People who smoke can drink 1/2 cup of carrot juice every day to protect their lungs. Carrots also contain calcium, phosphorous,

Dayan Qigong
Specialty Foods

copper, iron, fluorine, boron, and other minerals. Other benefits from eating carrots are lower blood pressure, strengthening of the heart, and lower blood sugar level.

Carrots can be eaten raw, shredded and mixed with sesame oil, or made into juice. They can be cooked with other vegetables and meat or used in soups.

Dayan Qigong
Specialty Foods

JADE GREEN HOLDING TAIJI CENTER

Serves 4
Ingredients:
10 oz. Spinach
8 oz. Fresh white mushrooms small size
4 oz. Dried black mushrooms.
2 tbs. Grapeseed Oil
4 pcs. Ginger
2 Green onions cut into 2 in. slivers.
Lotus root powder or cornstarch for thickening
Sauce:
    1 tbsp. soy sauce (lite), salt, 1 tsp sugar, ½ c water

Wash the white mushrooms. Soak and wash the black mushrooms, then cook about 10 minutes to soften and cut in various sizes.

Heat oil. Stir fry the spinach. Add a little salt for flavor. Take out the spinach and arrange it like a wreath around the outer edge of a serving plate.

Heat oil, add 2 pieces of ginger, some green onion, add black mushrooms and 2/3 of the sauce and let it stew for 5 minutes. Arrange this "dark side" inside of the spinach wreath.

Heat oil. Add 2 pieces of ginger, green onion, and small white mushrooms. Cook with the last 1/3 of sauce and stew for 2 minutes. Remove and arrange this "white side" inside the other half of the spinach wreath. The colors can be formed into the "Taiji" form.

Tomato and Eggs

Serves 4
Ingredients:
1 Tomato (about 32 oz.)
4 Eggs (organic)
2 tbs. Green Peas – frozen or fresh
3 Green Onions
1 tsp. Salt or to taste
4 tbs. Grape seed Oil
Boiled carrots for decoration

Cut the tomato into 1 inch squares.

Scramble the eggs.

Chop the green onions.

Add Grape seed oil in a pan and heat. Add eggs and scramble. Add onions, peas, and the tomato, folding the eggs over the tomato. When cooked (eggs are firm), place on a serving platter.

Decorate with cut boiled carrots.

PIPA TOFU "VIOLIN"

Serves 4

Ingredients:
2 lg. Packages of Medium firm Tofu with water removed
3 tbs. Starch (Cornstarch or tapioca starch)
3 Egg Whites
3 tbs. Gou Ji Zi (Fructus Lycium) - soaked in cold water and chopped lightly
2 tsp. Salt
1 tsp. White pepper

Break the Tofu into some pieces and squeeze in a piece of cheese cloth. This takes the water out of the Tofu. For vegetarians, tofu is the protein like meat. Mix the ingredients together and form into patties like Pea Ba (a violin like instrument in China)
Deep fry in oil.

Sauce
2 tbs. Sweetened lotus root powder
1 tbs. Vegetable soup base
2 tbs. Soy sauce (lite)
2 tbs. Grape seed oil
Little salt for flavoring
Little sugar for flavoring

4 pcs. Ginger
1 tbs. Sesame Oil
2 Green onions chopped
¼ c Chopped cilantro
½ c Water (may need more if needed)

Cook 4 pieces of ginger in 2 tablespoons oil. Remove the ginger after it turns brown. Add the water, soup base, soy sauce, and lotus root powder. Come to a boil. Add sesame oil, green onion, a little chopped cilantro, and a little Gou Ji Zi.

Spoon sauce over the tofu patties for extra flavor and to add color.

BARLEY SOUP

Barley is useful for eliminating "wetness" from the body. This soup can be made with almost any vegetables, but not green vegetables that cook quickly (like greens). Some suggestions are: celery, onion, cabbage, carrots, daikon, potato or green beans.

Serves 4
Ingredients:
1 lb. Large barley
8 c Water
2 c Large chunks of mixed vegetables
4 Slices of Ginger root
1 tbs. Lite Soy sauce
1 tbs. Vegetarian soup base
Salt to taste
1 tsp. Sugar to balance the salt (can be omitted for diabetic patients)
1 tbs. Black sesame oil
White pepper to taste

Wash barley 3 times and cook it in a pot with 8 cups of water for 30 minutes. Add large chunks of mixed vegetables, ginger, soy sauce, soup base, salt and sugar. Cook until tender, about another 30 minutes. Add a little more water to the cooking, if the soup becomes low. When done, add black sesame oil and white pepper to taste.

Dayan Qigong
Specialty Foods and Recipes

Seaweed & Egg Flower Soup

Serves 4
Ingredients:
    Sauce:
2 pcs. Seaweed (Nori)
1 pkg. Soft Tofu or Silk tofu
2 Eggs
1 med tomato
2 tbs. Green peas – frozen
2 Green Onions – Green Part
6 c Water

½ tbs. Sesame Oil
1 tbs. Vegetarian Soup Base
½ tbs. Soy Sauce (lite)
2 tbs. Lotus Root Powder (or starch)
    in 3 tbs. water

Break the seaweed into pieces and add to boiling water.

Scoop out tofu into balls, using a spoon, or cut into small squares.

Cut the tomatoes into thin slice wedges.

Cut the green part of the green onion into one-quarter inch slices.

Add all to the boiling water, add the green peas as the last ingredient.

After the water comes to a boil again, beat the eggs and spoon over the soup.

Mix the sauce ingredients and add to the soup. Again bring to boil. Serve the soup in a big soup bowl or tureen.

Mushrooms, Tofu, and Cabbage Stew

Ingredients:
6 pcs. Black Shitake Dried Mushrooms soaked and rinsed with stems cut off, and sliced
1 box Tofu cut into square pieces
8 parts Napa Cabbage cut into 2 inch length pieces
2 tbs. Grapeseed oil
5 slices Ginger
2 Green onions cut into 1 inch pieces
5 oz. Daikon radish cut into bite sized pieces
4 oz. Mung Bean thread noodles soaked and cut
¼ oz. Black Wood Ear soaked in warm water for 10 – 15 minutes and cleaned and sliced
½ oz. Black Dried Vegetable – Angel Hair Seaweed
1 oz. Kombu – a Japanese Seaweed, soaked and cut into long strips and pieces.
Boiled carrots slices thin for decoration

Sauce: Salt to taste, 1 tsp. sugar, 4 tbs. to ¼ c soybean sauce, ½ tsp white pepper,
2 tbs. Sweet Chinese cooking wine (Shaoshing wine)

Cut Napa cabbage into 2 inch length pieces. Put in the bottom of a clay pot with the stem part down and the green part on the top. Cover the cabbage with boiling water. Cook on low heat.

Place half of the tofu on top of the cabbage.

Stir fry in grape seed oil sliced ginger, green onions, mushrooms, wood ear, and Kombu.

Make the sauce and add to the stir fry.

Add stir fry to the clay pot. Let it simmer until almost soft, and then add the carrots and daikon pieces. Add more water and tofu pieces. Simmer ½ hour to 40 minutes.

5 minutes before finished simmering, add mung bean noodles and Angel hair seaweed arranged in a Taiji symbol, half black and half white. Add some liquid over the top. Add salt to taste.

Dayan Qigong
Famous Quotes: Model for Healthy Living

The following quotation were translated from a poem by Dr. Sun Si Miao who lived during the Tang Dynasty:

"Speak less, think less, eat less. Then you can sleep less, naturally. This is the living wisdom of immortality…"

"Today people believe that to live well is to eat and sleep a great deal, not knowing that too much food can block the flow of Qi and too much sleep can confuse one's thoughts. Over-eating and too much sleep are to be avoided."

Ten Ways to Stay Healthy and Prolong Life
(From ancient Chinese way of thinking)

Massage face regularly to produce a healthy pinkish glow and smooth skin texture. Brush hair thoroughly with fingers to reduce stress and tension, clear thoughts, and reduce high blood pressure.

Exercise eye muscles--rotate eyeballs clockwise from left to right 9 times with eyes closed

Hands covering both ears, move head up and down 5-7 times to clear the mind. This can also cure dizziness.

Swallow saliva regularly to increase digestion and produce a healthy stomach and spleen.

Cover back and keep it warm to protect the Du Mai (Governing meridian) located along the vertebrae. The human back is a passage to one's health; that is why it is important to keep the back warm.

Massage abdomen regularly, especially after eating to induce digestion and reduce bloating and constipation.

Massage chest regularly with hands to increase circulation to the heart.

Speaking excessively will damage the Qi and energy. Speak less will save energy and Qi. Therefore, speak less to reserve energy.

Massage the body with hands to stimulate blood circulation. Massage the whole body in a motion as if washing or taking a bath.

Dayan Qigong
Famous Quotes: Model for Healthy Living

Grandmaster Yang Mei Jun projecting qi cloud above her head

Dayan Qigong
Showing Respect Towards the Teacher

According to Chinese philosophy, the highest level of martial arts is internal. Internal martial arts accords perfectly with the *Tao*; it is a synergy of the body and mind. It is subtle and refined, not based on brute force or strength. To reach this level of achievement, the ancients have found it necessary to live a life grounded in virtue and deep respect.

A person studying the Tao respects all life—people, animals, flowers, trees. Even inanimate objects are respected—mountains, rocks, rivers, and so forth. Many trees and mountains have been around much longer than we have.

When studying martial arts, it is important to develop virtue, respect, and kindness. Being respectful is not weakness; on the contrary, it shows the strength of one's character and will deepen the development of one's martial arts.

To facilitate the nourishment of one's virtue, it is extremely important to learn the proper etiquette when learning with a teacher.

Addressing your teacher

When coming to the studio, the first thing is to acknowledge the teacher, your *Lao Shi*. Approach your teacher and, with your left palm covering your right fist (or simply placing your palms together), say one of the following:

- *Lao Shi Zao* if it is morning time. It is equivalent to saying "good morning teacher."
- *Lao Shi Hao* if it is at other times. It is equivalent to saying "wishing the teacher well"
- *Lao Shi Zai Jian* is used to say goodbye to your teacher. It means "see you again."
- *Lao Shi Wan An* means "good night teacher."

If you are a disciple of a teacher, you may simply address the teacher as "Lao Shi," or if the teacher is a male, "Shifu." To use the teacher's last name, e.g., "Chiang Shifu" or "Liu Lao Shi" is generally for the public or when you need to refer to the teacher in a speech or letter to a third party.

When studying from a teacher, make every effort to learn the teacher's name, biography, and lineage.

Dress

When coming to class, one sign of respect is to wear the uniform and to be well-groomed.

Table Etiquette

When at a dinner table, wait until the teacher sits before you sit. Serve tea to the teacher before serving to other students. The serving order is usually the teacher, older guests, younger guests, and finally yourself. Wait for the teacher to drink before one takes the first drink. At all times, ensure that the teacher has sufficient tea in his or her cup. If the teacher pours tea to you, at the very least, hold your cup with both hands. To be even more polite, you may stand up and hold the tea cup in both hands. Also, when giving a gift to the teacher, always present the gift with both hands.

When the meal arrives, wait for the teacher to eat before the student eats. One should make an effort to serving food to the teacher. When taking food, always give the "good stuff" to the teacher. The principle is that the student sacrifices a little for the sake of his or her teacher.

At the table with the teacher, refrain from talking with other students, especially while the teacher is talking. Instead, focus your mind, observe, listen, and learn. This provides an ideal atmosphere for the teacher to give further instructions. Remember, not everything is taught during formal class time.

After class, offer to clean the teacher's cup and wash all the dishes. After drinking tea, wash your own cup; never let the teacher clean up after you.

Traveling

When traveling, do your best to ensure comfort for your teacher. When walking, always walk behind the teacher except to open the door. When entering a place, let the teacher go in first; however, the student should knock on the door on behalf of the teacher.

Traditionally, the student should arrive to the studio first and leave last.

If the teacher is staying overnight at your house, provide the teacher with the best room.

In the Classroom

Listen carefully to the instructions and refrain from interrupting the teacher. You may ask questions at the appropriate time. Never ask the teacher to teach you something. The best is when the teacher imparts the knowledge without your asking.

If you are paying tuition, always pay on time and never let the teacher remind you. This is also a sign of respect.

Dayan Qigong
Showing Respect Towards the Teacher

When the teacher is teaching advanced movements specifically to another student, and if you are not on that movement, do not try to imitate the movements.

After learning something from the teacher, practice hard; otherwise, you have wasted the teacher's precious energy.

Master Hui Liu and Master Y. C. Chiang enjoying tea, 2004

Dayan Qigong
Testimonials

Tools for Daily Living By Gail Whang
When I excitedly and proudly told Master Hui Liu that I completed 1 full year of qigong... 365 days of continuous Qigong practice, she nonchalantly said, "Good, now do 1,000 days of practice. When you achieve that, Qigong will be fully integrated in your life."

On January 16, 2011, I completed my 1000th consecutive day of Qigong. Master Hui Liu's words are so true. Qigong has become an important part of my life. During this time I didn't miss a day of practice even though I traveled extensively throughout the world.

I have deep appreciation for my teachers, Master Hui Liu, Kirstin Lindquist and Cynthia Eaton. Kirstin inspired me and provided excellent and supportive instruction of the Dayan Wild Goose Qigong First Set. I was lucky to be a student in Master Hui Liu's last Second Set class and I am currently refining my practice in Cynthia Eaton's first / second set class. I would also like to acknowledge my practice group colleagues at Glenview School and Dimond Park for our daily practices, and my family who patiently supports me while I practice. And, finally, a special gratitude to the photographers who captured many Qigong moments in pictures throughout the world, Norm Gusner, Karl Gusner, Daniel Gusner, and Brenda Paik Sunoo.

Qigong has truly changed my life. Qigong was the first commitment I made upon retirement. Little did I know how this commitment would impact me. Before retirement I was an intense super-planner, demanding colleague and 24/7 multi-tasker workaholic. Qigong helped me slow down and gracefully ease into retirement. When I first started taking classes, in spite of Kirstin's encouragement, I struggled to practice at home. It wasn't until after 7 months of classes that I took up Kirstin's 100 day challenge... practice every day for 100 days in a row in order for Qigong to become a habit.

During this time, my husband and I traveled to France and Portugal. I was on Day 76 of my challenge. If I missed a day, I would have to start at Day 1 again. So, having a goal to complete the 100 days gave me the determination to overcome my self-consciousness when doing qigong at the airport and in public places. In fact, each day began with the purpose of finding a peaceful and scenic place to do my daily Qigong practice. My husband consulted his maps and scoped out a park, a vineyard, or on top of a scenic view area and off we went. Qigong taught us to slow down and appreciate the surrounding beauty.

Physically, I feel healthy and strong. I am more flexible than any time in my life, increasing my stretch by 12 inches. Qigong has also given me the confidence to self-heal my various aches and pains without relying on drugs and doctors. Two years ago I experienced sharp pains in both knees, which have healed through this gentle practice.

Perhaps the most telling aspect about the effects of Qigong on me is the observation from my son. When he sees me, he claims to know whether or not I've done my Qigong practice. "Mom, you didn't do Qigong today, did you?" He says when he feels I'm not listening attentively. He's most often correct. According to him, I am a better listener, more present and relaxed. He tells me that I am much more enjoyable to be with.

I am becoming much more accepting toward things that used to bother me and cause me a lot of grief. I have learned about the power of energy. I find myself focusing on positive energy and consequently generating positive energy. .

Qigong is teaching me about patience, especially toward learning. Three years and 8 classes later, I am still refining the movements of the first set. I am learning to be patient with myself as I work through and refine the movements. I am finally starting to internalize the notion that learning is a lifelong process and not a quick fix.
I am learning balance in my life and in my everyday activities. Learning to be more mindful and present is still an ongoing challenge for me, but through Qigong, I now have tools.

By Jan Targhetta

I was diagnosed with arthritis, fibromyalgia, asthma and lived with pain and painful spasms. I have been attending Dayan Qigong classes off and on since 2007. Approximately two years ago I noticed more flexibility and was finally able to practice the 1st set. I had also noticed that when I could not exercise I wasn't as flexible and my spasms were more painful.

Last year my asthma was out of control and I was not allowed to exercise for about five months. I started exercising again and then had a relapse. However, I realized that my old pains and very painful spasms re-occurred and I wanted to reduce the spasms and pain. It also helped that I do the Form while seated on a stool as I cannot stand for very long.

So this time I started doing the Form very gently so there would be no coughing and problems breathing. I told my Asthma Care Manager that I would do these exercises and nothing else until my asthma was under control and she gave her okay.

Last year I went to Denver and had no trouble adjusting to the altitude, and that was true again this year. Prior to learning qigong my body had great difficulty adjusting to Denver's high altitude and I had trouble breathing. I believe that my body is adjusting more quickly to the shift from sea level to Denver's high altitude more easily these days because of Dayan Qigong. I am actively working on developing qigong as a daily practice now. At the moment I am up to 82 consecutive days and counting. I can move more freely. It is easier to get up from a seated position. I feel more flexible and I have very few painful spasms.

I believe that because I learned 1st Set Dayan Qigong my quality life is much improved and I look forward to ongoing improvements.

Dayan Qigong
Testimonials

Jerry Pimentel, Embracing Health & Wellness Holistically

I was born 80 years ago into a large family of 17 siblings, on a plantation on the Island of Maui. I am the 16th child, and the 12th son. So I received of a lot of hand-me-downs. Coming from a large Portuguese family is like living within our own private community. Each of us was instilled with important values, an appreciation of education, and a respect for the need to cultivate a spiritual life. Our heritage also taught us that the family is the anchor of our lives.

Over the years I have been very fortunate to travel to many continents and countries, enjoying people of all walks of life and their specialties of food and wine.

In 1994 I had a problem with cancer. I learned about the benefits of Macrobiotic eating and food preparation, and decided to focus on making those fundamental lifestyle and dietary changes to address my health issues, rather than surgery. I became vegan for 4 years, and the doctors were amazed to see that the cancer cells were being exterminated simply by the changes in my eating habits. I am convinced that macrobiotics saved my life. I recovered from the cancer, and continue to be cancer free to this day. Along the way, I learned to enjoy cooking, and I found better health and peace of mind.

I have been practicing Dayan Qigong since 2005 and it has improved the quality of my daily life. I've learned how to let go of stress by meditating and doing the Form consistently. I feel calmer about most things these days, and do not seem to be as negative as I once was. I have more patience, and I experience more of an inner peace on a daily basis. I have better concentration, and it feels as if my brain is functioning better. I find that practicing Wild Goose Qigong three times a week with fellow students helps to keep my practice fresh and spirited.

I also enjoy swimming at the Hayward Plunge and hiking California trails. In May 2011, I completed a journey through the National Parks of the Western USA, driving and hiking along the way. Staying fit takes strength and energy.

What Dayan Qigong Has Given Me Despite Myself by Meltem Narter

When I got hurt in a traffic accident I had been studying Aikido. I was learning to merge with qi coming my way and to redirect it before it could hurt me. Before that, I had seven years of Shuri Ryu karate training, up to brown belt level. The disciplines had introduced me to mind, body, and spirit harmony, balance, and interconnectedness, and to Buddhism and meditation. After the accident and resulting brain injury, I couldn't practice martial arts, not even Tai Chi Chuan. I was so angry at the universe for delivering such an unfair and undeserved blow, that I wanted to kick and punch. I was distinctly aware of what I had lost, and was trying to find a replacement for my martial arts studies.

I was fresh out of a wheelchair, couldn't walk without stumbling, and my moves were pretty jerky. Since my balance was highly compromised, the only local martial arts teacher put me in touch with a qigong teacher named, Judy Shields. Judy's approach is very gentle and she introduced me to Dayan Qigong, which has become instrumental in my healing and growth in surprising ways.

Dayan Qigong found me at a time in my life when I didn't know how to get unstuck and move forward. Despite my interest in qi practices, and seeking balance between my mind, body, and spirit, I now understand how my relationship to life had been pretty unbalanced. I had always been more comfortable with the Yang aspect of who I am, both in my professional life and my social life. Because I loved to live with the illusion of control, life was never an adventure to relax into. It was full of jobs to be completed and conquests to be made.

While learning 1st Set through private instruction, I was also going to the Acquired Brain Injury Program at Coastline Community College, a daily cognitive and psycho-social retraining program for people like me with brain injuries. Early each morning before leaving home, I practiced the whole form with Master Hui Liu leading on the VHS. And every morning for almost a year, I finished my practice by bowing back to Shimu and smiling back to her in gratitude.

While I was doing all that, I had high expectations that the study of Dayan Qigong would give me what Western Medicine could not. I wanted my brain to function like before, I wanted my professional life back, to be able to drive again, and to be seizure free. So I practiced Dayan Qigong with a vengeance. I demanded that my brain remember the postures it was refusing to remember, instead of relaxing into the practice and just being with it. The book did not exist back then, and with my memory gone, I was taking lots of notes with sketches, so I could practice the form from week to week.

But I wasn't getting the results I wanted. It was no wonder that qigong wasn't helping me heal—I wasn't practicing with compassion for myself. Finally, after just a few 2nd Set sessions with Cynthia Eaton, and maybe due to my own personal growth, I finally heard the instructor's gentle encouragement to be non-judgmental with ourselves, to explore our range of motion and abilities with a sense of curiosity and compassion, to appreciate what we "can" do, rather than to obsess about what we cannot. I decided to practice with this new awareness and see where it might take me.

The brain injury cracked my protective Yang shell, so I could see the identities living inside. It was the practice of Dayan Qigong that enabled me to meet the gentler Yin aspect of myself. I began to make peace between my Yin and Yang energies. Now my balance and strength has improved enough that I am able to start practicing Tai Chi Chuan again, along with Dayan Qigong.

It was only after I started learning the 2nd Set, and started practicing meditative postures very slowly, that I was able to feel joy and able to allow my heart to be pierced by the exquisite beauty, especially when we practice in the park surrounded by gorgeous trees. I allow my imagination to connect me to the earth and feel the energy traveling up my legs, keeping me grounded. As I breathe in my surroundings, I am overcome by the feeling of joy and gratitude, as I stand amid and part of such a beautiful cross section of life. As I

breathe out, I become one with all that I see. How was I to know Dayan Qigong could open the door to such momentary bliss for such an ordinary, imperfect person like myself. How do I carry this awareness into my daily life?

By Connie Larsen

I started taking qigong classes because my Dad had passed away and I was depressed and I knew that some kind of exercise would be helpful. I found the Qigong class in a flyer at Kaiser Fremont. I went to the March 2008 demonstration class with Edith Chiang, and I knew immediately that this was just what I needed. I have been taking Dayan Qigong classes at Kaiser Fremont with Edith Chiang, and Kaiser Union City with Cynthia Eaton ever since.

Right away, learning the 64 movements helped improve my mood and concentration. Qigong has improved my flexibility and balance. I am much more limber, I can reach further, twist and turn more. It has also improved my strength and stamina. Now if I have to do a big job in the garden or house, I have the strength to finish the job.
Learning to meditate has been great for me, I feel able to handle everything that comes my way. I love to practice qigong with the friends I have met at classes. My Monday 5pm and Saturday 9am practice groups are the perfect way to start the week and the weekend.

Qigong brings me a lot of joy. I am so thankful to have learned it. I really appreciate my teachers who are so generous with their time and knowledge.

I started Qigong almost 3 years ago because I had injured my right wrist. It was bothering me for a year. Since doing Qigong, I have had no recurrent problem. Shimu keeps reminding me to soften and open my hands and the best angle for my arms and it has really been helping.
6 months after starting I seriously injured my left knee. Now 1 ½ years later, when I stand and hold knee in warm up and go down on one leg, the injured leg feels much better. The whole form feels very balanced and I feel stronger for doing it. My hands are starting to feel warm. It works well with Eutony.

Dayan Qigong
Testimonials

February 7, 1999

I feel the mind is sufficiently collected to make possible. Learning – that seems to occur 'in the body'. Trusting that what isn't known becomes known through the practice. The atmosphere created leaves room to learn in this way and at the pace dictated by whatever is my capacity at that moment. I feel better after class.

Health benefits – my energy seems greater. The healing with chi as we did it this morning seemed to change the sensation in the chest.

The repetition in some of the movements seems to create an inner rhythm, a pleasure in doing it and as if the "Reality" of 'Looking for food' becomes known.

I am quieter after class. I often do not wish to speak but remain in that inner quiet. Watching Shimu is for me a meditation.

I thank you.

Qigong makes a difference for my health:
1. My feet and hands are cold less and less often.
2. I never could breathe through my nose, now I can.
3. My complexion is clearer.
4. I've lost 10 lbs. – that may also be due to a vegetarian diet and lots of exercise.
5. My ankles are much firmer and stronger.
6. My memory is better long term and short term.
7. My brain thinks more clearly and with greater focus.
8. I rarely get sick and if I do it's for a short period and not very intense.
9. My face is changing, becoming more balanced on each side and having a more cheerful expression.
10. I have little pain or stiffness in my neck or shoulders.
11. I can sing in a higher key.
12. I am more mentally and emotionally stable, healthy and happy.
13. I have greater success in my business and personal relations so my stress level is lowering.
14. I have more energy and strength throughout the day.
15. I've quite smoking cigarettes.
16. I'm quitting drinking coffee.

---

1. Qigong has brought my blood pressure to 120/80; it was low before.
2. Before starting, it was suggested by an orthopedic surgeon that I have surgery on both shoulders and wrists. Qigong has increased my flexibility and the Qi moving through my meridians have helped my wrists and shoulders to the point that I don't need surgery.
3. My memory has improved.
4. Hand tremors have stopped – improved nervous system.
5. Most of the time I feel grounded – panics and anxiety are rare.
6. During meditation, answers to existing situations or problems come to me.

Dayan Qigong
Testimonials

7-14-99

I haven't had a cold or flu since I started the class a year and half ago – though I've been exposed to one or the other several times.

Before I started learning, I'd begun to have some trouble going back to sleep when I woke up in the middle of the night. (I'm 51) Early on, when I only knew the first part of the set, I began to visualize myself doing the form; I'd never get very far before I was asleep. This has meant that now I never worry about lying awake, because I know I won't have to, which probably means I sleep better overall.

I think I'm generally calmer than before I began. I feel I have "tools" that I can use if I feel stressed, and just that knowledge makes for less stress. For example, I've never liked flying much, and now I always do some massage and meditation while seated in the plane, and it really helps.

I no longer have a chronic stomachache I'd had maybe 1-4 times a month since college days. When, after 9 or 10 months of class, I learned that in "Pushing Forefoot" we were touching 2 points on the stomach meridian, I realized I hadn't had the stomachache all year!

Recently I've used my chi to help a friend who's recovering from foot surgery. In the days just following the surgery, she was in a lot of pain, and using a painkiller to ease it, but was still very uncomfortable. I just tried placing my palms near her foot, and from the first moment she felt results: warmth, tingling, and a feeling that there was internal movement. I could feel the heat and a buzzing, and later a pulsing of energy. I did it over a period of several days, and each time it gave her a great deal of relief.

1. I am much more limber.
2. I am a stronger, healthier person.
3. The chronic back pains and alignment problems I suffered in a car accident are gone.
4. I was able to keep myself out of surgery when I had a torn meniscus for a second car accident.
5. I see doctors and chiropractors less.
6. My stomach, legs and upper arm muscles are stronger.
7. My thighs and buttocks are less flabby.
8. I no longer feel "tethered" to my body.
9. I feel more "grounded" in my body.
10. I am more aware of my body space.
11. It is easier and feels better to attend to and follow my spirit, rather than my emotions.
12. I have fewer mood swings and I am no longer chronically depressed.
13. I am a calmer, content, less fearful person that I was when I first started practicing Qigong.
14. An intuition about balance between body, mind, and spirit is strengthening in me.
15. My shoulders are more relaxed.
16. I walk in the world more confidently.

Stress reduction, especially at work. Have some improvement in the immune system. Lungs clearing during 43 and 44. Clears the mind. Brings me back into my body when my spirits is having trouble grounding.

Dayan Qigong
Testimonials

Increased energy. Not getting sick. Need for less sleep, decreased digestive problems.

It is easier to fight off colds/flu's when I practice. I always feel an increased feeling of energy and well-being after practice.

I have more energy, higher sensitivity (feeling meridians open and chi moving), more tranquility, and easier concentration.
   After the philosophy or theory is explained, I understand the practice (beyond intellectual understanding) holistically and naturally. Everything feels as if it's fallen into its rightful place.

I feel stronger, more flexible.

1. Health Benefits since starting Qigong:
   a). Qigong has brought my blood pressure to 120/80, it was low before.
   b). Before starting it was suggested by an orthopedic surgeon that I have surgery on both shoulders and both wrists. Qigong has increased my flexibility and the Qi moving through my meridians have helped my wrists and shoulders to the point that I don't need surgery.
   c). My memory has increased.
   d). Hand tremors have stopped-improved nervous system and control.

2. The feeling of balance and harmony after practice.

3. Most of the time I feel grounded-panics and anxiety are rare.

4. During meditation answers to existing situations or problems come to me.

The *Form*, for me, is like a tune-up for a car. When I do the Form, I feel like I've just "booted-up" my computer. The *Form* makes me feel like I've just run my fingers through all the systems of my body...plucked all the strings, combed out my hair, freshened and refreshed everything in my body and all my body's sophisticated computer systems. The *Form* is like an exercise to set a tuning fork. Mediation is an exercise to calibrate the instrument of body and soul to the music of a grander design. The stronger our connection is, the more attentive we become in allowing our spirit to be guided. We worry less because we are less absorbed by the ordinary projections of our mind. The Form improves the functioning of the computer-who we are in the physical realm. Meditation improves the functioning of the form of who we are in spirit.

I honor you as my teacher and thank you for the opportunity to express myself privately in writing.

Dayan Qigong
Testimonials

Testimonials from Kirstin Lindquist's students

Thank you so much for your Qigong practice, which has changed my life. When I came to class two years ago I was so weakened from chronic fatigue syndrome and fibromyalgia that I had to sit most of the time. Now I practice the form daily! I'm no longer in bed for five days at a time from pain but am only dysfunctional one day now and then. I owe you and Kirstin so much for my healing!
-Suzanne Lavoie

Thank you forever for teaching/guiding Kirstin who taught/guided me and introduced me to daily practice (the 1000-day challenge). I now am "practicing more" as you suggest-daily-. The day is not right without practice. And I am perhaps going on 1000 days, which is wonderful and also small when I think of the time you've practicing. Again Shimu, thank you and Master Yang and Dayan Qigong.
-Sid Sattler

Immense gratitude for the gift of practice.
-Peggy Bush

Feeling waterfalls ringing drawing our centers long. Thank you for helping me find CENTER.
-Karen J.

Thank you so much for this Qigong practice it brings much peace and serenity to my life.
-A.P.

My gratitude for the life giving gift of this practice. With each practice find more strength, clarity and appreciation for the moment.
-C. D.

I came to Qigong after a serious fall which hurt my back. It has not only helped me heal but has brought more joy and health t my life. Thank you so much.
-Suzie McLean

The best way to live in the moment. Thank you for bringing this form of Qigong to us.
-Ian McDonald

Wonderful to have an energy community alive and active in Oakland. Appreciation!
-Nona Hungate

We enjoy the camaraderie and the Chi while practicing at Lake Temescal on Sunday mornings. It is so special having a Qigong -tai chi community during these transforming times in the USA and the world.
-April McDonald

Dayan Qigong
Testimonials

When I began taking Kirstin's Qigong class three years ago, it was at a point of severe depression in my life. The practice, the benign and helpful teaching, and the growing community have been a source of healing and strength training for me. Now there are times every day when I feel Qi moving me. Thank you very much for planting these precious seeds in the world.
-Sara Katz

Your lovely painting mirrors qigong practice- graceful, tranquil and profound. Thank you for bringing Dayan qigong to the Bay Area.
-Wendy Rosner

Additional testimonials:

1. I didn't get easily tired.
2. I need less sleep.
3. My body got lighter and my head clearer.
4. My back pain, caused by an old car accident is completely gone.
5. I am happier than before.
6. I have more positive thoughts.
7. I can endure the winter coolness a lot better.

Students practicing Dayan Qigong, 2004

Dayan Qigong
Scripts and Their Translations

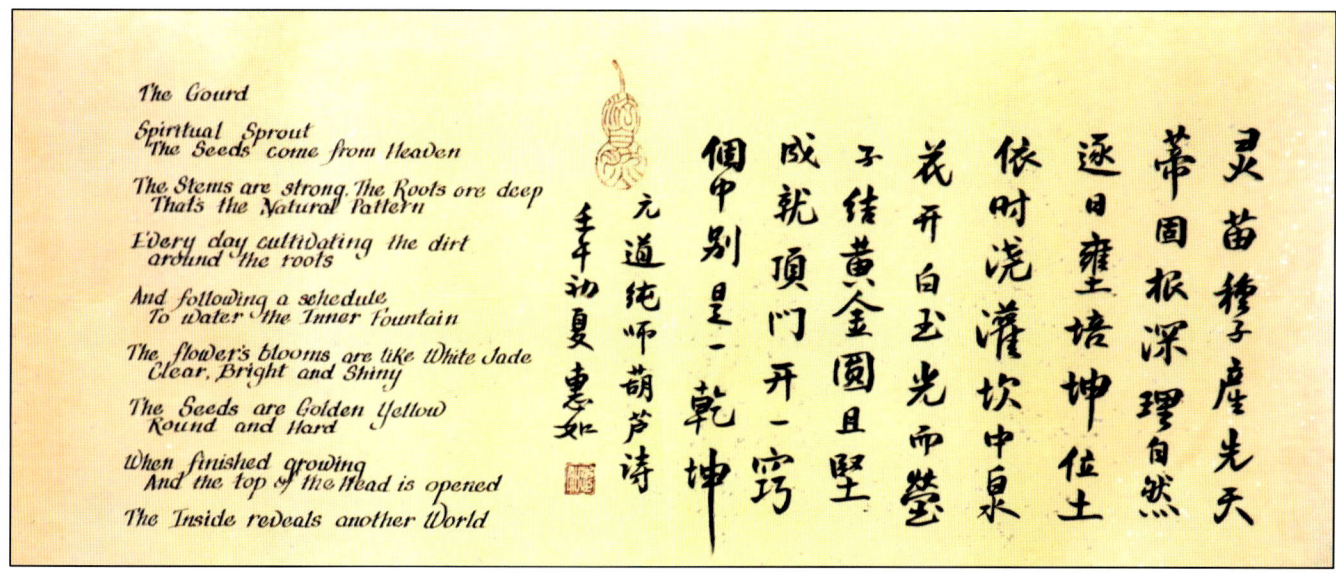

One who practices the Tao will achieve Tao. According to Grandmaster Yang, this is Dayan Qigong's "lineage verse" that has been passed down from many generations.

Giant Buddha in Sichuan Province

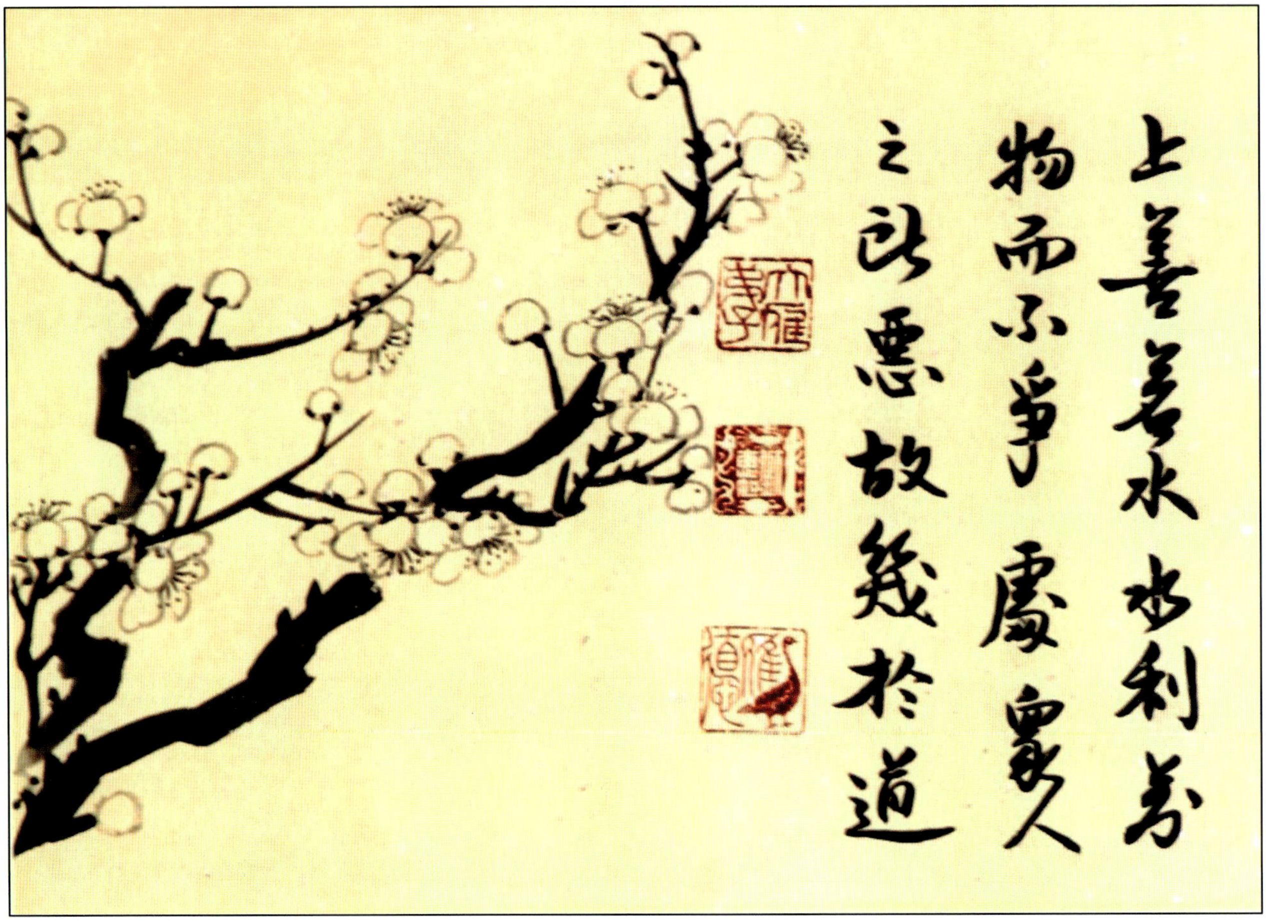

Dayan Qigong
Scripts and Their Translations

Dao De Jing (Verse 8)

Supreme goodness is like water,
Which nourishes effortlessly all things.
It flows to the lowest places people shun.
Hence, it is in harmony with the Great Way.

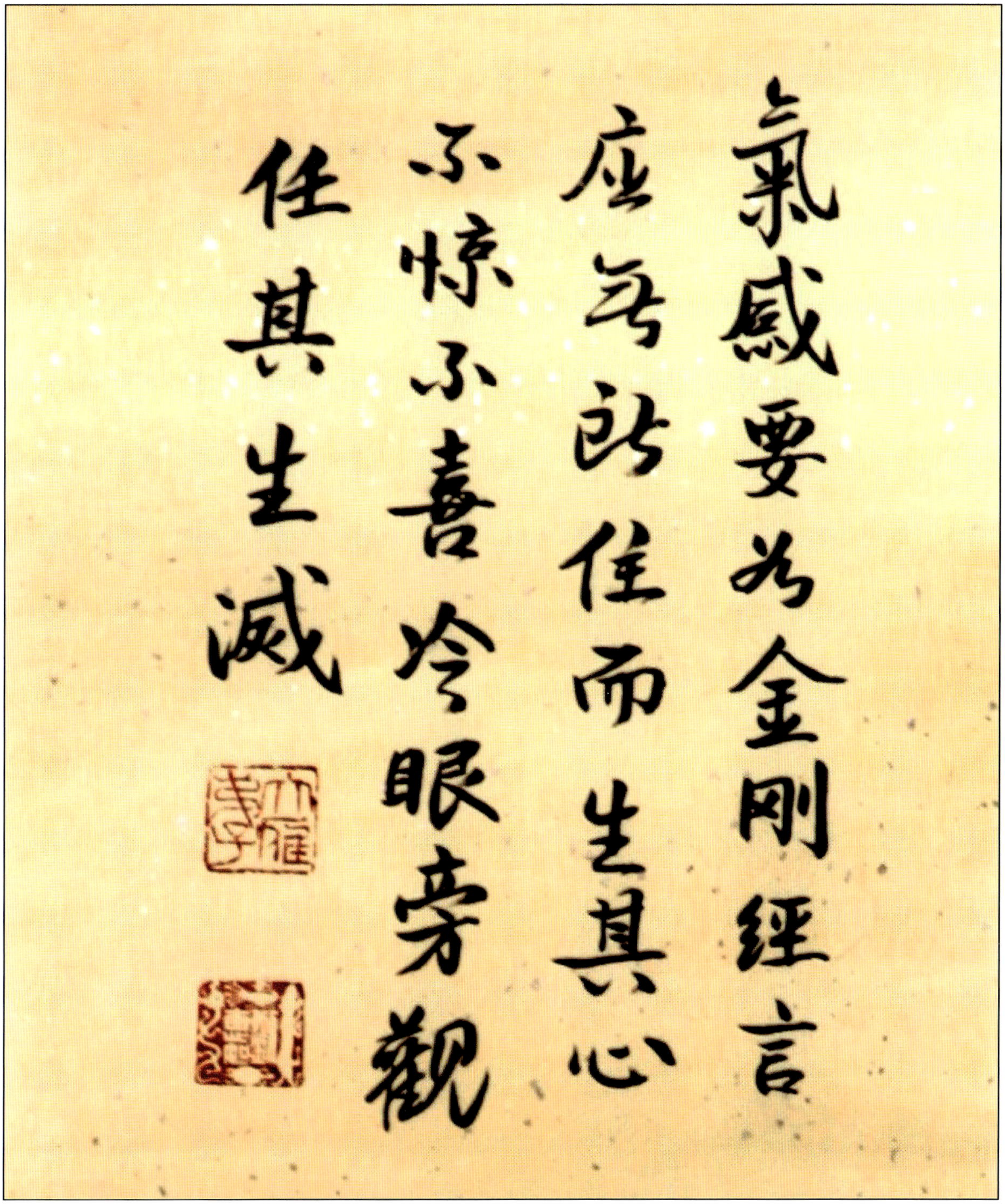

Dayan Qigong
Scripts and Their Translations

> 氣感要為金剛經言
> 應無所住而生其心
> 不驚不喜冷眼旁觀
> 任其生滅

Verse on Qi Sensations

The awareness of Qi sensations should accord with the teachings of the Diamond Sutra: "Without attaching to any place or thing, let your mind function freely." No surprises, no delight. Contemplate it with indifference, like an impartial bystander. Let it come, let it go.

Dayan Qigong
Scripts and Their Translations

甘露法語

人在哪裡，心在哪裡，專注、作主，就是真正的自在．

惟覺大和尚法語

Wherever you are, that is where the mind should be.
Always be mindful, and be your own master.
This is true freedom.

Words of Wisdom from Zen Master Wei Chueh

Dayan Qigong
Scripts and Their Translations

智者：能固守其精則陰陽俱益而筋骨強壯，

愚者：欲竭其精以耗散其真至半百而衰老矣！

The wise: He who completes his spirit through the balancing of Yin and Yang will become strong.
The foolish: He who wastes his spirit through trivial pursuits will appear broken and frail.

Dayan Qigong
Scripts and Their Translations

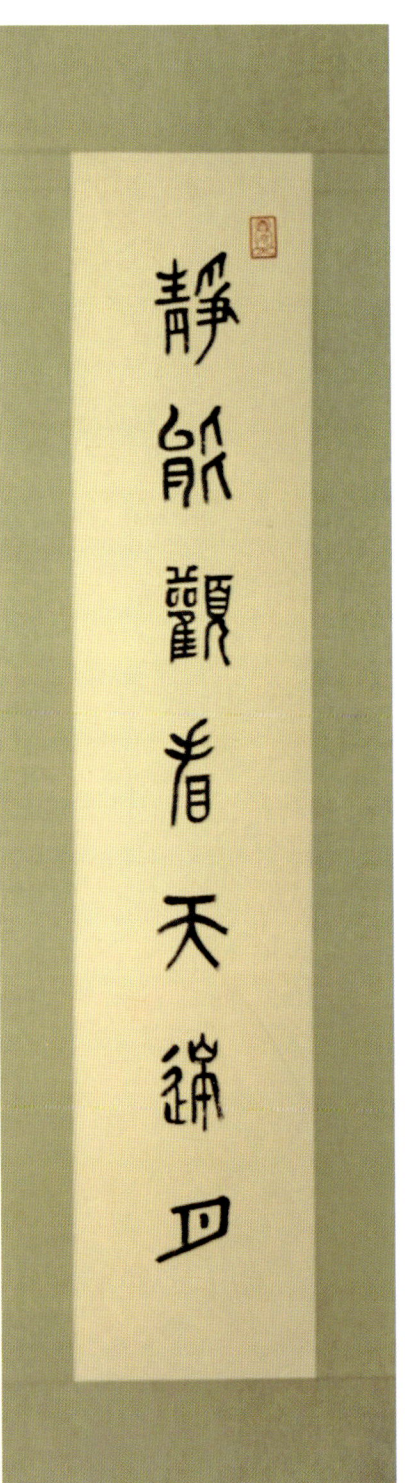

Internal calmness yields universal vision,
In stillness the pearl can be found in the deep ocean,
Through Zen contemplation one arrives at quietude, serenity, wisdom, and bliss.